THE AUTHORITY
OF THE BELIEVER

FOUNTAIN OF LIFE
THEOLOGICAL INSTITUTE INTERNATIONAL

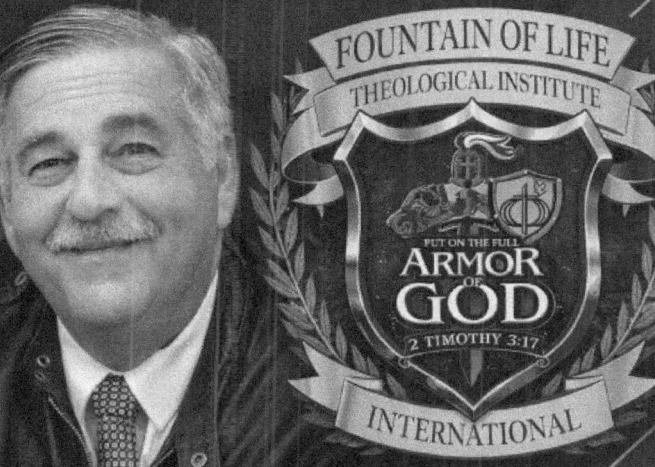

DR. GREG WOOD

COURSE SYLLABUS

The Authority of the Believer
Course Level: Bible College / Seminary
Credit Hours: 3
Language: English
Instructor: Dr. Greg Wood
Institution: Fountain of Life Theological Institute International

COURSE DESCRIPTION

This course explores the biblical foundation, spiritual principles, and practical applications of the believer's authority in Christ. Students will learn how to exercise dominion over sin, sickness, and the powers of darkness, as well as how to operate effectively in spiritual warfare, intercession, and victorious Christian living. Emphasis is placed on scriptural understanding, identity in Christ, and practical ministry application.

COURSE OBJECTIVES

By the end of this course, students will be able to:

1. Explain the scriptural basis for the believer's authority through Christ.
2. Understand the believer's position and identity in the new creation.
3. Identify areas where the authority of the believer must be exercised.
4. Demonstrate the authority of the Word and the Name of Jesus in daily life and ministry.
5. Develop confidence in prayer, proclamation, and spiritual warfare.
6. Minister with authority in deliverance, healing, and intercession.

COURSE REQUIREMENTS

- Attendance and participation in lectures
- Weekly reading assignments and scripture study
- Midterm and final written examinations
- Practical ministry exercise in prayer and declaration
- Final paper: *"Exercising Spiritual Authority in Ministry and Daily Life"*

KEY SCRIPTURES

- Luke 10:19
- Ephesians 1:17–23; 2:4–6
- Colossians 2:10–15
- Mark 16:17–18
- Matthew 28:18–20
- James 4:7

INSTRUCTOR'S NOTE

This course is designed to move believers from mere theological understanding to dynamic, Spirit-empowered living. Authority is not theoretical; it is meant to be *exercised* in prayer, proclamation, and spiritual dominion.

THE AUTHORITY OF THE BELIEVER
A Comprehensive Syllabus and Course Manual
Dr. Greg Wood
Fountain of Life Theological Institute International

© 2024 Dr. Greg Wood

All Rights Reserved. No portion of this syllabus may be reproduced or transmitted in any form without prior written permission from the author or the International Theological Institute Fuente de Vida.

Edition: 1st Edition

Language: English

Published by: *Fountain of Life Theological Institute*

Dedication

To all believers who dare to rise in faith, walk in dominion, and enforce the victory of Christ on earth.

This work is lovingly dedicated to the men and women of God who refuse to live beneath their inheritance and who know that through Christ, we reign in life.

Dr. Greg Wood

Acknowledgments

I wish to express my deep gratitude to the Holy Spirit, the divine Teacher, who continually opens the Scriptures and reveals the reality of our authority in Christ Jesus.

Special thanks to the faculty, students, and ministry partners of **Fountain of Life Theological Institute International**, whose passion for truth and ministry excellence makes this work possible.

A sincere word of appreciation to the countless ministers, teachers, and intercessors across the world who have walked in and demonstrated the believer's authority through their lives of faith and obedience.

To all my colleagues, mentors, and students - you are the living testimony that *"greater is He that is in you, than he that is in the world."*

Preface

The subject of **The Authority of the Believer** is not new, but it is often neglected or misunderstood. Many Christians live as though powerless, unaware of the spiritual authority granted to them through the finished work of Christ.

This course aims to restore that understanding and to awaken the Church to her true position in Christ Jesus.

The believer's authority is not arrogance; it is alignment with divine order. It is standing in the delegated power of Jesus Christ, enforcing the victory already won at Calvary. When the Church realizes her position in Him, hell trembles, prayer becomes powerful, and ministry becomes fruitful.

In this syllabus and accompanying manual, you will explore Scripture after Scripture, precept upon precept, learning how to apply spiritual authority in prayer, healing, deliverance, and daily life.

This material is both academic and experiential - it invites you not only to learn about authority, but to **walk in it.**

"Behold, I give unto you power to tread on serpents and scorpions, and over all the power of the enemy: and nothing shall by any means hurt you."

(Luke 10:19)

May every student and minister who studies these pages rise in boldness, discernment, and dominion through the indwelling Christ.

Dr. Greg Wood
Founder and President
Fountain of Life Theological Institute International
Contact:
info@fountainoflifemx.org
www.fountainoflifemx.org

CHAPTER 1 - THE ORIGIN OF AUTHORITY

"Let them have dominion..." – Genesis 1:26

Introduction: The Missing Revelation

Many Christians live as though they were spiritual victims—buffeted by fear, temptation, and defeat - when in fact, they were designed to reign with Christ. The truth of the believer's authority is one of the most vital, yet most neglected doctrines in the body of Christ.

Authority is the *foundation of Kingdom operation*. Without it, faith becomes timid, prayer becomes uncertain, and spiritual warfare becomes ineffective. To understand authority, we must return to the beginning, to God's original design in creation, the loss of dominion through sin, and the restoration through Christ.

> "You will never walk in what you do not understand; and you cannot exercise what you do not know belongs to you."

This chapter traces the story of **divine authority** from the throne of God, to the creation of man, to the tragic fall, and to the prophetic promise of restoration through Jesus Christ.

1. God's Eternal Seat of Government

Before there was time, there was **throne**. Before creation, there was **sovereignty**.

Psalm 103:19 declares:

"The LORD has established His throne in the heavens, and His kingdom rules over all."

This means God's rulership is not a reaction - it is eternal. The universe itself was born under divine law and sustained by divine order. Authority flows from the **throne of God**, not from human ability.

The Nature of Divine Authority

- It is **absolute** - not subject to vote or negotiation.
- It is **righteous** - His authority expresses His holiness and justice.
- It is **benevolent** - God's authority is always exercised for the good of creation.

God's authority governs the cosmos: stars, seasons, and nations. His decrees are binding; His Word is law. All true authority in heaven and earth is **delegated**, never original except in God Himself.

> "Authority is not something God has—it is who God is."

2. Humanity's Created Dominion

Genesis 1:26–28 is the first record of human purpose:

"Then God said, 'Let Us make man in Our image, according to Our likeness; let them have dominion... over all the earth.'"

This verse establishes **man's identity** and **assignment** in one statement. Humanity was created to be **the visible expression of the invisible God** - a steward of creation under divine authority.

The Hebrew Understanding

The Hebrew word for *dominion* (רָדָה — *radah*) means "to rule, to manage, to govern, to tread down."

It does not mean domination or oppression. It means *management under commission*.

Man was made in **God's image (tselem)** meaning moral, spiritual, and intellectual resemblance - and **God's likeness (demuth)** meaning functional representation.

In other words, **man was God's representative governor on earth**.

Illustration:

A king's statue placed in a conquered territory symbolized his reign. Likewise, humanity is the "image" of God placed in the earth as proof of Heaven's sovereignty.

The Mandate of Dominion

God blessed Adam and Eve and said:

"Be fruitful and multiply, fill the earth and subdue it; have dominion..." (Genesis 1:28)

The verb *subdue* (בָּכַשׁ - *kabash*) implies bringing order, cultivating potential, and extending the boundaries of divine order into the material world. This was humanity's mission: to make the earth a reflection of Heaven.

3. The Harmony of Heaven and Earth

Originally, **Heaven and Earth were united**. Adam lived in unbroken fellowship with God. His words carried authority because they were perfectly aligned with God's will. He named the animals not by invention but by revelation.

In Eden, man functioned as the **spiritual governor** of the physical realm.

His spirit ruled his soul; his soul ruled his body; and together, man ruled creation under God.

This order mirrored Heaven's government: God → man → creation.

Disobedience would invert that structure, causing chaos and death.

> "When man obeyed God, creation obeyed man."

4. The Catastrophe of Rebellion

The tragedy of Genesis 3 is not merely the eating of forbidden fruit, but it is also the **abdication of authority.**

When Adam and Eve disobeyed, they transferred their dominion to another spiritual master.

Romans 6:16 explains:

> *"Know ye not, that to whom ye yield yourselves servants to obey, his servants ye are to whom ye obey;"*

By choosing Satan's word over God's, man came under Satan's rule. The serpent became *"the god of this world"* (2 Corinthians 4:4), holding authority not by right but by *usurpation*.

This act fractured creation's order:

- Spirit was dethroned.
- Soul took dominance.
- Body succumbed to corruption.

The Legal Transfer

Satan's authority became **legal**, because man, the lawful steward, willingly yielded his rights. Authority on earth belongs to whoever holds the title deed - and Adam handed it over.

> "Disobedience is not just sin, it is treason against divine government."

From that moment, fear replaced faith, shame replaced glory, and chaos entered creation.

5. The Prophecy of the Seed

Yet, immediately after the fall, God revealed His redemptive plan. **Genesis 3:15** declares:

> *"I will put enmity between you and the woman, between your seed and her Seed; He shall bruise your head, and you shall bruise His heel."*

This verse, known as the **proto-evangelium** (the first Gospel), is the announcement of a coming Redeemer.

The "seed of the woman" points prophetically to **Christ**, born of a virgin, who would crush the serpent's head - the symbol of authority.

Through this promise, God declared a *spiritual counterattack*. The authority lost through Adam's disobedience would be reclaimed through Christ's obedience.

Theological Insight:

The entire Bible is the unfolding of Genesis 3:15. From Eden to Calvary, Scripture narrates God's quest to restore divine authority in human hands.

6. The Covenant Pattern of Restored Authority

Throughout the Old Testament, we see glimpses of restored authority through covenant relationship:

Covenant Figure	Type of Authority	Scriptural Reference
Noah	Authority through righteousness	Genesis 6–9
Abraham	Covenant authority through faith	Genesis 12–22
Moses	Mediatorial authority through divine commission	Exodus 3–14
David	Kingly authority through anointing	1 Samuel 16–2 Samuel 7
The Prophets	Vocal authority through revelation	Jeremiah 1:10; Ezekiel 2:7

Each covenant built anticipation for the Messiah, the **ultimate covenant representative**, who would exercise perfect authority over sin, death, and the devil.

7. Authority: A Principle of Representation

Biblically, authority always functions through **representation**. Adam represented humanity; Christ represents the redeemed. **Romans 5:17** teaches:

> *"For if by one man's offense death reigned through the one, much more those who receive abundance of grace... will reign in life through the One, Jesus Christ."*

This verse defines the essence of authority: *to reign in life.*

The word *reign* (Greek: βασιλεύω - *basileuō*) means "to rule as a king." The believer's authority is not futuristic; it begins now, because we share in Christ's position of dominion.

8. Understanding Authority and Power

In the New Testament, two Greek words clarify this dynamic:

- **Exousia** (ἐξουσία) *authority, jurisdiction, legal right.*
- **Dunamis** (δύναμις) *power, ability, miraculous strength.*

Authority is the *legal right to act*; power is the *ability to enforce that right*.

Jesus operated in both, and He conferred both upon His disciples (Luke 9:1).

> "Authority is delegated position; power is divine enablement. When the two unite, Heaven moves."

A believer who understands authority but lacks power will struggle.

A believer who has power but no revelation of authority will misuse it.

The mature Christian walks in **balanced dominion**- legal right empowered by divine might.

9. The Silence of Adam: A Lesson in Abdication

Notice that in Genesis 3, Adam was **present** during Eve's temptation but remained silent.

He failed to exercise the very authority entrusted to him.

The serpent's words should have been rebuked, not reasoned with.

Key Insight:

Authority ignored is authority surrendered.

This same passivity cripples many believers today. The enemy still speaks lies, and silence still gives him space.

When the believer refuses to speak the Word, the serpent still whispers in the garden.

> "You cannot rebuke what you continue to tolerate."

10. Jesus Christ: The Restorer of Authority

Christ came as the **Second Adam** (1 Corinthians 15:45).

Where the first Adam failed through disobedience, Jesus triumphed through obedience.

He faced Satan not in a garden of abundance but in a wilderness of lack and won.

At Calvary, Jesus fulfilled Genesis 3:15. His heel was bruised, but the serpent's head or his authority—was crushed.

Colossians 2:15 proclaims:

> *"Having disarmed principalities and powers, He made a public spectacle of them, triumphing over them in it."*

In His resurrection, authority returned to its rightful place - under the feet of the redeemed.

> "The Cross was not only about forgiveness; it was about the restoration of dominion."

11. The Legal Foundation of Believer's Authority

Matthew 28:18-19 records the triumphant decree:

> *"All authority has been given to Me in heaven and on earth. Go therefore..."*

This *"Go therefore"* transfers the operational authority to the believer.

The believer now acts *in the Name of Jesus* - a legal commission backed by the throne of Heaven.

Theological Principle:

Authority is never earned through effort; it is received through identification with Christ.

Ephesians 2:6 affirms:

"And He raised us up together, and made us sit together in the heavenly places in Christ Jesus."

You are not fighting for victory, you are enforcing victory already won.

12. Living Under Authority to Walk in Authority

True authority flows only from submission. Even Jesus said,

"I do nothing of Myself; but as My Father taught Me, I speak these things." (John 8:28)

Rebellion forfeits authority; humility secures it. The centurion in Matthew 8:9 understood this when he said,

"I am a man under authority, having soldiers under me..."

He recognized that authority is both **positional and relational** - you must be under it to operate in it.

> *"You cannot cast out what you still agree with; authority begins with obedience."*

13. The Restoration Mandate

Through redemption, the believer now carries Heaven's governmental commission:

- To **subdue** spiritual opposition.
- To **speak** the Word of God in faith.
- To **release** the Kingdom in every environment.
- To **represent** the King in character, not just in command.

Authority is not arrogance, it is alignment.
It is not about control, it is about spiritual order.

The believer becomes an ambassador of divine government in a fallen world.

14. Reflection and Discussion

1. How does the concept of *delegated authority* redefine your understanding of ministry?
2. Why must authority always be rooted in submission to God's Word?
3. In what areas of life have believers abdicated their rightful authority?
4. How can prayer, confession, and obedience restore divine order?
5. What does it mean to "reign in life" through Christ (Romans 5:17)?

15. Practical Ministry Exercise

Assignment:

Lead students in a declaration service. Have each one stand and verbally renounce the spirit of passivity and fear.

Then read aloud the following **Dominion Declaration:**

"I am created in the image of God.

I am redeemed by the blood of Jesus.

I am seated with Christ in heavenly places.

I have authority over sin, sickness, and Satan.

I reign in life through the One, Jesus Christ.

I will not live beneath my inheritance.

I walk in victory, boldness, and divine dominion. Amen."

Chapter Summary

- Authority originates in God's eternal throne.
- Humanity was created as Heaven's representative on earth.
- The fall transferred authority to Satan.
- God's redemptive plan through Christ restored dominion.

THE AUTHORITY OF THE BELIEVER

- The believer now enforces that victory by faith and obedience.
- True authority flows from submission to divine order.

Key Scripture for Memorization
"Behold, I give you authority to trample on serpents and scorpions, and over all the power of the enemy, and nothing shall by any means hurt you."
Luke 10:19

CHAPTER 2 - THE TRIUMPH OF CHRIST

"Having disarmed principalities and powers, He made a public spectacle of them, triumphing over them in it." – Colossians 2:15

Introduction: The Centrality of the Cross

The Cross is not merely the symbol of Christianity; it is the **courtroom of eternity**. There, justice and mercy met; righteousness kissed peace (Psalm 85:10).

Through the obedience of Christ, every legal claim that sin and Satan held over humanity was canceled, and the authority forfeited by Adam was **legally restored**.

The resurrection was not the end of the story, but rather a **public declaration** that the verdict had been rendered: *Christ reigns, the devil is defeated, and the believer is free to reign again.*

> "The Cross was the battlefield; the Resurrection was the victory parade."

1. The Need for a Perfect Redeemer

The fall placed humanity under the dominion of sin and death. Because authority was lost legally, it had to be **restored legally**. Only a man could reclaim what a man had lost; yet only God could pay the price of redemption.

Thus, the Redeemer had to be both **fully divine** and **fully human.**

- As man, He could stand as humanity's representative.
- As God, His righteousness could satisfy divine justice.

Scripture Foundation:

"For there is one God and one Mediator between God and men, the Man Christ Jesus." **1 Timothy 2:5**

Jesus was not born through Adam's corrupted seed but through divine conception - the *seed of the woman* promised in Genesis 3:15. His humanity made Him legal on earth; His divinity made Him powerful enough to redeem.

2. The Incarnation: God Enters the Battlefield

In the incarnation, God stepped into human history not as a distant judge, but as a **combatant-Redeemer**.

Philippians 2:6-8 reveals that Christ *"made Himself of no reputation, taking the form of a bondservant."*

By becoming flesh, He entered the enemy-occupied territory. Yet unlike Adam, He lived in perfect obedience. Every temptation was an opportunity to maintain Heaven's authority in human form.

Illustration:

Satan offered Jesus all the kingdoms of the world (Matthew 4:8-10). Ironically, those kingdoms were rightfully His - but only through the path of obedience, not compromise.

> *"Where the first Adam surrendered authority through disobedience, the Last Adam secured it through submission."*

3. The Ministry of Christ: Demonstration of Dominion

Every miracle of Jesus was a **manifestation of recovered authority**.

THE AUTHORITY OF THE BELIEVER

- He **spoke to storms** (Mark 4:39).
- He **commanded demons** (Mark 1:27).
- He **forgave sins** (Mark 2:10).
- He **healed the sick and raised the dead** (John 11:43).

These were not random acts of compassion only; they were **governmental acts** - signs that the Kingdom of God had re-entered the world through a Man under divine authority.

Key Verse:

"If I cast out demons by the Spirit of God, surely the kingdom of God has come upon you." **Matthew 12:28**

Each act of power was a declaration: *The authority Adam lost has returned through the Son.*

4. The Substitutionary Sacrifice

The Cross represents a **legal exchange**. Christ bore our sin, shame, and judgment, satisfying every demand of divine justice.

2 Corinthians 5:21 declares:

"He made Him who knew no sin to be sin for us, that we might become the righteousness of God in Him."

At Calvary, the spotless Son became the substitute sinner so that sinners might become sons.

Satan's greatest weapon - guilt was destroyed when the sin-debt was paid in full.

> "Where justice demanded payment, mercy provided the Lamb."

When Jesus cried, *"It is finished!"* (John 19:30), the Greek word *tetelestai* meant *"paid in full."* The ransom was complete, and Hell's claim was void.

5. The Descent and Triumph

Between death and resurrection, Scripture reveals that Christ descended into the realm of the dead - *Hades* to proclaim His victory.

Ephesians 4:8-10 says:

"He descended into the lower parts of the earth... that He might fill all things."

1 Peter 3:19 describes Him *"preaching to the spirits in prison."* This was not an offer of salvation but a **proclamation of victory.**

Colossians 2:15 summarizes it:

"Having disarmed principalities and powers, He made a public spectacle of them, triumphing over them in it."

The ancient world understood a *triumph* as a Roman victory parade - the defeated enemies dragged in chains behind the conquering general. The resurrection of Christ was Heaven's **Triumphal Procession.**

> "Hell heard His footsteps before the stone was rolled away."

6. The Resurrection: Proof of Dominion

Romans 1:4 declares that Jesus was *"declared to be the Son of God with power... by the resurrection from the dead."*

The resurrection was Heaven's endorsement of His authority.

Death, the final tyrant, was dethroned.

"O death, where is your sting?

O Hades, where is your victory?" **1 Corinthians 15:55**

Every other world leader dies and remains in the grave; only Jesus **rose in triumph**.

That single event became the **legal evidence** that all authority had been reclaimed.

Illustration:

The empty tomb is not merely an artifact of history; it is the divine receipt stamped across eternity: *PAID - VICTORY SECURED.*

7. The Ascension and Enthronement

After forty days of post-resurrection ministry, Jesus ascended to Heaven and was seated at the right hand of the Father - the position of ultimate authority.

Ephesians 1:20-22 describes this enthronement:

"He raised Him from the dead and seated Him at His right hand... far above all principality and power and might and dominion."

This seating signifies **rest and rule**. His work of redemption is finished, and His authority is absolute. From that position, He intercedes for His people and governs His Church.

> "The Cross gave Him the crown; the Throne proves His reign."

8. The Transfer of Authority to the Church

Immediately following His declaration,

"All authority has been given to Me in heaven and on earth" (Matthew 28:18),

Jesus commissioned His disciples:

"*Go therefore...*"

The phrase *"Go therefore"* is the hinge of delegated authority. It implies: *Because I have it, I now authorize you to use it in My Name.*

Mark 16:17-18 confirms this:

"In My name they will cast out demons... they will lay hands on the sick, and they will recover."

Authority is transferred through the **Name** of Jesus.

This is not a magical formula but a legal empowerment. The believer stands as Christ's representative, backed by Heaven's government.

9. The Legal Nature of Redemption

The Cross is both **a battlefield** and **a courtroom**.

Legally, Jesus satisfied divine justice. Spiritually, He destroyed demonic power.

Colossians 2:14 states that He *"wiped out the handwriting of requirements that was against us."* In ancient law, a canceled debt was marked *tetelestai* - "paid in full."

The believer no longer battles for forgiveness; the verdict has been rendered: **Not guilty — justified by faith.**

Key Principle:

The authority of the believer stands on **legal redemption**, not emotional experience.

> "You cannot defeat the enemy by emotion, but only by revelation of what is legally yours."

10. The Triumph Over Satan

Satan's defeat was **total** and **public**.

His weapons of accusation, deception, fear, and death - were rendered powerless.

Hebrews 2:14 says:

"Through death He might destroy him who had the power of death, that is, the devil."

The Greek word for *destroy* (*katargeō*) means "to render inoperative, to make powerless."

Satan still operates, but only through deception; his power exists only where ignorance persists.

> "The devil's only weapon now is a lie; his only strength is your ignorance."

When believers stand in their identity in Christ, the enemy has no jurisdiction.

11. The New Covenant Position of the Believer

Christ's triumph positioned every believer **in Him**.

Ephesians 2:6 declares:

"He raised us up together and made us sit together in heavenly places in Christ Jesus."

This is the believer's *legal position*.

We are not merely servants pleading for victory, we are sons and daughters enforcing a victory that has already been won.

Our prayers are not earth-to-Heaven cries, but Heaven-to-earth decrees.

We do not fight *for* authority; we operate *from* authority.

> "The believer's warfare is enforcement, not negotiation."

12. The Triumph Manifested in the Church

Acts 3 and Acts 16 show the continuation of Christ's authority through His followers.

- Peter and John said to the lame man: *"In the name of Jesus Christ of Nazareth, rise up and walk."*
- Paul commanded the spirit of divination: *"I command you in the name of Jesus Christ to come out of her."*

These were not prayers for power; they were **decrees of authority.** The early Church understood its legal right to act as Heaven's agents on earth.

The same authority is available today - but it must be activated by faith, obedience, and revelation knowledge.

13. Living in the Power of His Triumph

To live in Christ's triumph is to maintain a **victory mentality.**

Romans 8:37 says:

"In all these things we are more than conquerors through Him who loved us."

The phrase *"more than conquerors"* translates *hupernikaō* - "to be overwhelmingly victorious."

It means we fight battles already decided in our favor.

Key Concept:

- Faith enforces victory.
- Worship celebrates victory.
- Obedience sustains victory.

> "The cross defeated Satan once; our confession enforces it daily."

THE AUTHORITY OF THE BELIEVER 25

14. Reflection and Discussion

1. Why was it necessary for the Redeemer to be both divine and human?
2. How does understanding the legal nature of redemption strengthen spiritual warfare?
3. What does Christ's resurrection prove about the believer's position?
4. How does the phrase *"Go therefore"* redefine the mission of the Church?
5. What practical steps help a believer walk daily in Christ's triumph?

15. Ministry Application
Class Exercise:

Have students identify areas of personal defeat and replace them with victory declarations.

Example:

- *Defeat thought:* "I am weak."
- *Declaration:* "I can do all things through Christ who strengthens me."

Lead the class in a prayer of triumph:
"Lord Jesus, You conquered sin, death, and the grave.
Your victory is my victory.
I stand in Your authority and reject every lie of the enemy.
I decree freedom, healing, and dominion.
The same Spirit that raised Jesus from the dead lives in me.
I walk in Your triumph today and every day. Amen."

Chapter Summary

- The Cross legally restored man's authority.
- The Resurrection validated the victory.
- The Ascension enthroned Christ above all powers.
- The Church now carries delegated authority through His Name.
- The believer enforces, not negotiates, the triumph of Christ.

Key Verse for Memorization

"And He put all things under His feet, and gave Him to be head over all things to the church, which is His body, the fullness of Him who fills all in all."
Ephesians 1:22–23

CHAPTER 3 - THE BELIEVER'S POSITION IN CHRIST

"And hath raised us up together, and made us sit together in heavenly places in Christ Jesus." Ephesians 2:6

Introduction: Knowing Where You Stand

Authority flows not from emotion, but from **position**. Many believers attempt to fight the enemy from the wrong location — from earth, rather than from Heaven's vantage point.

Your *spiritual position* determines your *spiritual authority*.

When a believer understands their position *in Christ*, fear loses its grip, prayer gains confidence, and victory becomes a daily reality. This chapter unveils the mystery of the believer's exalted place in Christ; not as theory, but as truth to be lived and enforced.

> *"You will never rule over what you do not stand above."*

1. Seated with Christ: The Revelation of Position

Paul's letter to the Ephesians unveils a divine truth hidden from ages:

"God... raised us up together, and made us sit together in heavenly places in Christ Jesus." (Ephesians 2:6)

This is not future tense — it is **completed tense**.

When Christ was raised, the believer was *legally included* in His resurrection and enthronement.

Positional vs. Experiential Reality

- **Positional truth** is what God declares as accomplished.
- **Experiential truth** is how we live it out by faith.

You may still walk on earth, but spiritually you are seated with Christ at the right hand of the Father — a place of dominion, peace, and delegated authority.

Key Concept:
Position precedes power; revelation precedes manifestation.

2. Identification: The Secret of Union

The believer's authority depends on **identification** — understanding that everything Jesus did, He did *as us* and *for us*.

Romans 6:3–5 reveals the mystery:

> *"Do you not know that as many of us as were baptized into Christ Jesus were baptized into His death?... that just as Christ was raised from the dead... even so we also should walk in newness of life."*

This means:

- When Christ **died**, we died *with Him*.
- When He **was buried**, we were buried *with Him*.
- When He **rose**, we rose *with Him*.
- When He **sat down**, we sat down *with Him*.

This is not poetic; it is **positional substitution.**

Our identity has shifted from Adam to Christ; from defeat to dominion; from bondage to blessing.

> "Christianity is not self-improvement; it is identity replacement."

3. The Exchange at the Cross

At Calvary, the greatest spiritual exchange in history took place:

Jesus Took	So We Might Receive
Our sin	His righteousness
Our shame	His glory
Our poverty	His abundance
Our sickness	His healing
Our rejection	His acceptance
Our death	His life
Our defeat	His victory

Isaiah 53:5-6 and 2 Corinthians 5:21 summarize this redemptive exchange.

Through it, the believer becomes the righteousness of God - not by works, but by grace through faith.

You no longer stand as a guilty sinner begging for mercy, but as a restored heir seated in heavenly authority.

> "The Cross was the exchange table where the guilty became kings."

4. The Believer's Legal Position

Christ's authority is not His alone, but it is shared.

Ephesians 1:20-22 declares that He is seated "far above all principality and power."

Then Ephesians 2:6 says *we are seated with Him.*

This means we share His jurisdiction over demonic powers, spiritual wickedness, and the curse of sin.

Our prayers are not from below begging for help; they are from above enforcing His victory.

Heavenly Places Defined

The phrase *"heavenly places"* (Greek: *epouranios*) does not mean distant galaxies; it refers to the *spiritual realm of authority*. It is where decisions are made, decrees are issued, and dominion is exercised.

You are positioned there - not by merit, but by union.

> *"Authority is not earned through struggle but accessed through seating."*

5. The Mindset of the Seated Believer

Position without mindset produces defeat. Many Christians are *seated* legally but still *crawl* mentally.

To reign with Christ, your thoughts must align with your seat.

Colossians 3:1-2 commands:

> *"If you then were raised with Christ, seek those things which are above... Set your mind on things above, not on things on the earth."*

The believer must think like royalty, not like refugees.

This is not pride; it is perspective.

Your seat determines your speech. Your identity determines your authority.

Illustration:

A king sitting on his throne does not shout to prove authority; he simply issues a decree. Likewise, the believer does not plead; he proclaims.

> *"Kings don't beg. They decree."*

6. The Believer's Spiritual Inheritance

Ephesians 1:11 says, *"In Him also we have obtained an inheritance."*

This inheritance is not postponed to Heaven; it begins now — peace, healing, dominion, wisdom, and authority in Christ.

You are not a beggar waiting for Heaven's charity; you are a co-heir of Heaven's treasury.

Romans 8:17 confirms:

"And if children, then heirs; heirs of God, and joint-heirs with Christ;"

Everything that belongs to Christ legally belongs to you relationally.

> "Our inheritance is not what we earn from God, but what we share with Christ."

7. Standing in Righteousness

Authority requires righteousness. Guilt paralyzes faith; righteousness empowers it.

Proverbs 28:1 says, *"The righteous are bold as a lion."*

Righteousness gives you the right to stand before God without fear and before the devil without shame.

2 Corinthians 5:21 declares:

> "Boldness in prayer is not arrogance—it is awareness of righteousness."

"He made Him who knew no sin to be sin for us, that we might become the righteousness of God in Him."

You are not "becoming" righteous... you *are* righteous in your new nature. Authority flows from this identity.

8. Dominion Over the Old Nature

Although the believer is seated in Christ, the old carnal nature still seeks to dominate. **Romans 6:12** commands,

"Do not let sin reign in your mortal body."

Authority begins with **self-government**.

You cannot rule spiritual atmospheres if you are ruled by emotional impulses. Dominion begins internally before it is exercised externally.

Key Principle:

- Master your mind.
- Govern your tongue.
- Discipline your desires.
- Align your actions with your position.

> "The first throne a believer must conquer is the heart."

9. Authority Over Circumstances

Romans 5:17 says,

"Those who receive abundance of grace and of the gift of righteousness will reign in life through the One, Jesus Christ."

To *reign in life* means to rule over circumstances, not be ruled by them.

This authority is not domination over people but dominion over adversity.

Believers command peace in storms, not panic; declare provision in lack, not fear. Authority is expressed through faith-filled words anchored in God's promises.

> *"Your confession is the determining force of your dominion."*

10. The Believer's Authority in Prayer

Prayer from the position of being seated with Christ changes everything.

Instead of pleading from earth, you legislate from Heaven.

Intercession becomes decree. Petition becomes enforcement.

Matthew 18:18 declares:

"Whatever you bind on earth will be bound in heaven, and whatever you loose on earth will be loosed in heaven."

This is judicial language. The believer is Heaven's ambassador, declaring divine verdicts.

Illustration:

The courts of Heaven respond not to emotion but to jurisdiction. When you pray in Jesus' Name, you are exercising *divine jurisdiction*.

> *"Prayer is not begging God to move; it is enforcing what He has already decreed."*

11. Walking in Daily Awareness of Position

Authority is sustained by **awareness**.

You cannot exercise what you forget.

Every morning, the believer must renew his consciousness: *"I am in Christ, and Christ is in me."*
John 15:5 affirms:

"He who abides in Me, and I in him, bears much fruit; for without Me you can do nothing."

Abiding keeps you aligned with your authority.
You don't visit your position occasionally - you live from it permanently.

> *"Awareness of position produces assurance in authority."*

12. Hindrances to Walking in Authority

There are three primary enemies that undermine positional authority:

Hindrance	Description	Remedy
Ignorance	Not knowing who you are in Christ	Study and revelation
Condemnation	Feeling unworthy of authority	Rest in righteousness
Passivity	Failing to act on truth	Faith and obedience

> *"Authority unused is authority lost."*

13. The Corporate Position of the Church

Ephesians 1:22–23 calls the Church "His body, the fullness of Him who fills all in all."

This means the Church is Christ's continuing presence and power on earth.

Our collective authority is multiplied through unity and agreement.

Where the individual believer has jurisdiction, the corporate Church has *territorial dominion*.

When the Church prays, preaches, and worships in unity, the gates of hell cannot prevail.

> "The Body of Christ is God's governmental presence in every generation."

14. Reflection and Discussion

1. What does it mean to be "seated with Christ"?
2. How does identification with Christ redefine your sense of self?
3. In what ways does righteousness empower boldness?
4. How can believers learn to pray from the position of authority rather than need?
5. What internal attitudes hinder the exercise of authority?

15. Practical Ministry Exercise
Class Practice:

Have each student write and declare ten *"In Christ"* confessions (e.g., "I am complete in Christ," "I am seated with Him," "I reign in life through Jesus Christ").

Follow with a time of corporate declaration, affirming the believer's position over fear, sickness, and spiritual oppression.

Prayer Declaration:

"Father, thank You for seating me with Christ in heavenly places.
I live from victory, not for victory.
I am hidden in Christ and clothed in righteousness.
I reign in life through Jesus Christ my Lord.
I refuse fear, defeat, and condemnation.
I walk in my divine position every day. Amen."

Chapter Summary

- The believer's authority flows from being *in Christ*.
- We are seated with Him - legally enthroned in the spirit.
- Identification with His death, resurrection, and seating defines our victory.
- Authority begins with inner dominion and expands outward.
- Awareness of position is the foundation of confidence in prayer and warfare.

Key Verse for Memorization

"If anyone is in Christ, he is a new creation; old things have passed away; behold, all things have become new."
2 Corinthians 5:17

CHAPTER 4 - THE NAME OF JESUS

"Therefore God also has highly exalted Him and given Him the name which is above every name." Philippians 2:9

Introduction: More Than a Word

The Name of Jesus is not a charm, a religious formula, or a phrase we attach to the end of prayers. It is **the legal and spiritual representation of the person, power, and authority of Christ Himself.**

When you speak that Name in faith, Heaven recognizes it, Hell trembles at it, and creation responds to it. The believer's authority operates through the revelation of this Name.

> "When you use His Name, it is as though Jesus Himself were speaking."

1. The Origin of the Name

The angel Gabriel declared to Mary:

"You shall call His name Jesus, for He will save His people from their sins." **Matthew 1:21**

The name *Jesus* (Greek: **Iēsous**, Hebrew: **Yeshua**) means **"Yahweh saves"** or **"The Lord is salvation."** It embodies both the mission and the nature of Christ.

From the moment of His incarnation, that Name carried Heaven's authority, but it was **through obedience and victory** that it became exalted above all others.

Philippians 2:8–9 explains:

"He humbled Himself and became obedient to the point of death... Therefore God also has highly exalted Him and given Him the name which is above every name."

The Name was not merely given - it was **bestowed through conquest.**

> *"The Cross was the battlefield where the Name was crowned with power."*

2. The Authority Behind the Name

Authority always depends on **the power behind it.**

A police officer's authority comes not from his uniform, but from the government backing that uniform.

Likewise, the believer's authority in the Name of Jesus carries the full weight of Heaven's throne.

Three Dimensions of Christ's Authority

1. **Inherited Authority** – as the eternal Son (Hebrews 1:4).
2. **Bestowed Authority** – as the obedient Servant (Philippians 2:9).
3. **Conferred Authority** – as the risen Lord who delegates it to the Church (Matthew 28:18-19).

When the believer invokes the Name, all three dimensions are in operation.

3. The Legal Right to Use the Name

Jesus explicitly transferred the legal right to use His Name to those who believe in Him.

> *"Whatever you ask in My name, that I will do."* **John 14:13**
> *"In My name they will cast out demons."* **Mark 16:17**

THE AUTHORITY OF THE BELIEVER

In Greek, the phrase *"in My name"* (*en tō onomati mou*) literally means **"in My authority, on My behalf."**

It is a legal signed authorization empowering the believer to act as Christ's representative.

Illustration:

When an ambassador speaks in the name of a nation, his words carry the authority of that nation. In the same way, when you speak in the Name of Jesus, Heaven itself stands behind your words.

> "The Name of Jesus is the believer's signature of Heaven."

4. The Power Demonstrated Through the Name

Throughout Scripture, the Name of Jesus consistently brought visible results:

- **Healing:** *"In the name of Jesus Christ of Nazareth, rise up and walk."* **Acts 3:6**
- **Deliverance:** *"I command you in the name of Jesus Christ to come out of her."* **Acts 16:18**
- **Salvation:** *"Whoever calls on the name of the Lord shall be saved."* **Acts 2:21**
- **Boldness:** *"They spoke the word of God with boldness."* **Acts 4:31**

These were not magic incantations; they were **legal commands** backed by revelation. The early Church had no fear because they knew the Name they carried.

> "Demons recognize authority more quickly than many believers do."

5. The Revelation of the Exalted Name
After the resurrection, Jesus said:
"All authority has been given to Me in heaven and on earth. Go therefore..." **Matthew 28:18-19**
This was the moment of **transference.**
The Name of Jesus became the operational instrument through which the Church would exercise the dominion of Heaven on earth.
Ephesians 1:21 describes His exaltation:

> *"Far above all principality and power and might and dominion, and every name that is named."*

That phrase "every name that is named" includes every sickness, fear, addiction, curse, or demonic title that can be spoken. The Name of Jesus outranks them all.

> "Every name must bow to the Name of Jesus."

6. Using the Name in Prayer
Prayer in the Name of Jesus is not merely adding words to the end of a request - it is praying *as His representative.*
When you pray in His Name:

- You stand in His righteousness.
- You speak with His authority.
- You access the Father's throne as if Jesus Himself were asking.

John 16:23-24 says:

"Whatever you ask the Father in My name He will give you... Ask, and you will receive, that your joy may be full."

This means your prayer carries **His access, His favor, and His endorsement.**

> *"Prayer in the Name of Jesus turns petitions into decrees."*

7. Using the Name in Spiritual Warfare
The enemy recognizes only one authority - the Name of Jesus.
Luke 10:17 records,
"Lord, even the demons are subject to us in Your name!"
The believer does not fight Satan with emotion or volume, but with jurisdiction.

When the Name is spoken in faith, demonic resistance collapses under divine decree.

Acts 19:13-16 tells of Jewish exorcists who attempted to use the Name without relationship. The demons replied,
"Jesus I know, and Paul I know; but who are you?"
This shows that authority in the Name flows only from **relationship, revelation, and righteousness.**

> *"The devil knows whether your use of the Name is revelation or imitation."*

8. The Name as Our Covenant Seal
In Scripture, the Name represents **covenant ownership.**

Jeremiah 14:9 calls God *"the One whose name is called upon us."*

Likewise, believers are marked by the Name of Jesus; it is our covenant identity and protection.

"They shall see His face, and His name shall be on their foreheads."
Revelation 22:4

Every time you act, pray, or speak in His Name, you affirm that seal - you are declaring: *"I belong to Him, and He works through me."*

> "The Name of Jesus is the believer's badge of ownership and authority."

9. The Name and the Word

The authority of the Name is inseparable from the authority of the Word.

Psalm 138:2 says,

"You have magnified Your word above all Your name."

This means the Word validates the Name, and the Name activates the Word.

When you speak Scripture in the Name of Jesus, the decree becomes a two-edged sword empowered by both covenant and command.

> "The Word gives substance to the Name; the Name gives power to the Word."

10. The Limits of Authority in the Name

Authority in the Name of Jesus is powerful, but not autonomous. It is governed by:

THE AUTHORITY OF THE BELIEVER 43

1. **Alignment with God's will** - not personal agenda (1 John 5:14).
2. **Faith in the finished work of Christ** - not superstition.
3. **Obedience to the Word** - authority flows through submission.

The Name cannot be used for manipulation or self-exaltation. It functions only within the boundaries of divine purpose.

> "The Name of Jesus is not a tool for our will, but the voice of His."

11. Living Consciously in the Power of the Name

The revelation of the Name should shape every aspect of a believer's life:

- **In Worship:** We exalt His Name (Philippians 2:10).
- **In Prayer:** We approach the Father through His Name (John 16:23).
- **In Ministry:** We serve in His Name (Colossians 3:17).
- **In Warfare:** We overcome in His Name (Revelation 12:11).

<u>Colossians 3:17</u> sums it up perfectly:
"Whatever you do in word or deed, do all in the name of the Lord Jesus."

> "The believer's entire life is meant to be lived under the banner of the Name."

12. Reflection and Discussion

1. Why is the Name of Jesus the legal basis for spiritual authority?
2. How does understanding the Name change the way we pray?
3. What are some improper ways the Name of Jesus is used today?
4. How can believers cultivate deeper revelation of the Name?
5. What relationship exists between the Word of God and the Name of Jesus?

13. Practical Ministry Exercise
Class Activation:
Have each student write three declarations using the Name of Jesus over different areas of life (e.g., health, family, ministry).
Then lead a corporate decree service:
Prayer Declaration:
"Father, thank You for the power of the Name of Jesus.
I stand under its authority and speak with its power.
In the Name of Jesus, I command every force of darkness to bow.
I decree healing, provision, and victory in every area of my life.
The Name of Jesus is my authority, my access, and my triumph. Amen."

Chapter Summary

- The Name of Jesus embodies the full authority of Heaven.
- It was exalted through obedience and conquest.
- Believers have legal right to act in that Name.
- Demons, sickness, and circumstances bow to its command.
- The Name functions through relationship, revelation, and alignment with God's will.

Key Verse for Memorization
"And whatever you ask in My name, that I will do, that the Father may be glorified in the Son."

John 14:13

CHAPTER 5 - THE WORD OF GOD AS AUTHORITY

"For the word of God is living and powerful, and sharper than any two-edged sword." Hebrews 4:12

Introduction: The Word — The Constitution of the Kingdom

Every kingdom is governed by a **constitution**. The Kingdom of God is no exception; its constitution is the **Word of God**.

The Bible is not a mere record of divine thoughts but the *active covenant document* by which Heaven rules and earth aligns.

All spiritual authority flows from that Word - revealed, believed, and spoken.

> "The Word of God is the believer's bill of rights and sword of enforcement."

1. The Word as Final Authority
Psalm 119:89 declares,

"Forever, O Lord, Your word is settled in heaven."

God does not consult opinion polls; His Word is the unchanging decree of His government.

Because the Word is eternal, it outranks feelings, circumstances, and tradition.

Authority begins when the believer stops negotiating with emotion and starts standing on revelation.

Key Principle:

God's Word is not true because you believe it; it is true, therefore you believe it.

2. The Living Nature of the Word

Hebrews 4:12 describes the Word as *"living and powerful."*

The Greek term **zōn** (living) means "alive, active, energetic." The Word breathes with divine life.

When spoken in faith, it reproduces what it declares.

<u>Isaiah 55:11</u> promises:

"My word... shall not return to Me void, but it shall accomplish what I please."

> "Every verse is a seed; every confession is a harvest."

3. The Word and Creation

The entire universe was framed by God's spoken Word (Hebrews 11:3).

Genesis 1 repeats the phrase *"And God said"* ten times; ten decrees establishing creation's order.

The same creative force now operates in the believer's mouth when aligned with Scripture.

Illustration:

The sun still rises because God once said, *"Let there be light."*

Your circumstances will change when you say what He said.

4. Jesus — The Living Word Incarnate

John 1:1 – 14 reveals that Jesus Himself *is* the Word made flesh.

To honor the Word is to honor Christ; to reject the Word is to resist Him.

Authority in the Word is authority in the Person of Jesus, for He and His Word are one.

> "The power of the Word and the presence of Christ can never be separated."

5. The Word as Spiritual Weapon

Ephesians 6:17 calls Scripture "the sword of the Spirit."
When spoken aloud, it pierces darkness and silences accusation.
Jesus modeled this in Matthew 4:1-11, defeating Satan three times with the same weapon: *"It is written."*
Each declaration dismantled temptation's lie.
No argument in Hell can stand against *It is written*.

> "The Word in your mouth is as powerful as the Word in His mouth."

6. The Word and Faith
Romans 10:17:

"Faith comes by hearing, and hearing by the word of God."

Authority functions only through faith; faith functions only through the Word.
The more you hear the Word, the greater your conviction that what God said *is already done*.
Key Idea:
The Word produces faith; faith activates authority.

7. The Word as Legal Evidence
In a court, evidence decides verdicts.
In the courts of Heaven, the Word is the believer's *evidence* of covenant rights.

When you quote Scripture, you present legal precedent before the Judge of all.

Jeremiah 1:12 records:

"I am watching over My word to perform it."

Heaven enforces its own statutes.

> "The Bible is God's lawbook; prayer is the believer's courtroom."

8. The Power of Confession

Mark 11:23 teaches that whoever believes and *says* will have whatever he says.

Confession means "to say the same thing as God."

When your words agree with His, your mouth becomes Heaven's microphone.

Illustration:

A soldier's rifle has no power until the trigger is pulled; likewise, the Word stored in the heart is released through speech.

> "Silence cancels authority; confession activates it."

9. The Word and Obedience

Authority without obedience becomes hypocrisy.

James 1:22 warns, *"Be doers of the word, and not hearers only."*

Obedience establishes credibility in the spiritual realm. Demons know who actually practices the Word (Acts 19:13-16).

> "You cannot command what you refuse to obey."

10. The Word in Worship and Prayer

True worship is Word-based. God seeks worshippers who adore Him *in spirit and truth* (John 4:24).

When the Word fills worship, authority fills the atmosphere.

Likewise, praying Scripture transforms prayer from opinion to proclamation.

Example:

Instead of *"Lord, help me,"* declare, *"Lord, You are my refuge and strength (Psalm 46:1)."*

> "Worship exalts His presence; the Word defines His promises."

11. The Word and Spiritual Maturity

Hebrews 5:14 teaches that mature believers have "their senses exercised to discern both good and evil."

Spiritual maturity is not age - it is *Word saturation*.

Immaturity complains; maturity declares.

The depth of your Word determines the reach of your authority.

12. The Word and the Holy Spirit

The Spirit never operates apart from the Word.

He confirms what God has said, not what man imagines.

When you speak Scripture, the Spirit energizes it with creative power (John 6:63).

> "The Spirit is the breath; the Word is the sword—together they conquer."

13. Reflection and Discussion

1. Why must the Word be the believer's supreme authority?
2. How does speaking Scripture differ from positive thinking?
3. What practical steps strengthen your daily Word life?
4. How does obedience to the Word amplify authority in ministry?
5. In what ways can the Word be applied as legal evidence in prayer?

14. Practical Ministry Exercise
Assignment:
Have students select five promises of God and write corresponding decrees.
Each decree should begin with *"It is written."*
End the session with corporate declaration:
Prayer Declaration:
"Father, Your Word is my final authority.
I believe it, I speak it, and I live it.
It is written - I am more than a conqueror.
It is written - by Your stripes I am healed.
It is written - no weapon formed against me shall prosper.
I decree victory, peace, and dominion in Jesus' Name. Amen."

Chapter Summary

- The Word of God is eternal, living, and authoritative.
- It is both the constitution and the sword of the Kingdom.

THE AUTHORITY OF THE BELIEVER

- Faith and authority grow through hearing and speaking the Word.
- The Word must be believed, spoken, and obeyed.
- The Spirit and the Word operate together to enforce Heaven's will.

Key Verse for Memorization
"So shall My word be that goes forth from My mouth;
it shall not return to Me void,
but it shall accomplish what I please,
and it shall prosper in the thing for which I sent it."
Isaiah 55:11

CHAPTER 6 - THE BLOOD OF JESUS

"They overcame him by the blood of the Lamb and by the word of their testimony." Revelation 12:11

Introduction: Heaven's Most Powerful Evidence

From Genesis to Revelation, the scarlet thread of redemption runs unbroken. Every covenant, altar, and victory points to one unchanging truth - **without the shedding of blood there is no authority over sin, Satan, or death** (Hebrews 9 : 22).

The blood of Jesus is not symbolic sentiment; it is *spiritual legislation*. It purchased, sealed, and enforces every right the believer possesses.

> *"The authority of the believer rests on the legality of the blood."*

1. The Principle of Substitution

From the garden's animal sacrifice (Genesis 3 : 21) to Israel's Passover lamb (Exodus 12), God revealed that innocent blood must cover guilty man.

The blood is life (Leviticus 17 : 11). When life is given, sin's penalty is paid.

Christ fulfilled every shadow when He offered Himself once for all (Hebrews 9 : 12).

He became both the Priest and the Sacrifice - the One who offered and the One who was offered.

Key Idea: *The Cross was the courtroom where justice met mercy through blood.*

2. The Blood and Covenant

Every divine covenant is ratified by blood.

In the Old Testament, animal blood sealed temporary covenants; in the New, the blood of Jesus established an **eternal covenant** (Hebrews 13:20).

At the Last Supper He said,

"This cup is the new covenant in My blood, which is shed for you." Luke 22:20

The believer's authority therefore operates within covenant law - our rights are not demanded; they are *already signed in blood.*

> "The blood on the document is Heaven's signature of ownership."

3. The Blood and Redemption

1 Peter 1:18-19 says,

> "You were not redeemed with corruptible things...but with the precious blood of Christ."

The word **redeem** (Greek *lutroō*) means "to purchase back by paying a ransom."

Humanity's title deed, lost through Adam, was bought back at Calvary. The price was not silver or gold - it was divine life.

Illustration: A slave can never free himself; liberty demands an outside purchaser. Jesus paid not merely *for* us but *as* us.

> "The Cross was Heaven's marketplace where man was bought back and Satan lost the deed."

4. The Blood and Justification

Romans 5 : 9 proclaims,

"Having now been justified by His blood, we shall be saved from wrath through Him."

Justification is a legal term meaning *declared righteous, acquitted of all charges.*

Because of the blood, there is no record left to accuse us. The Judge Himself declares, *"Case dismissed."*

Key Principle: *You cannot reign in life while living under condemnation; the blood removes the evidence of guilt.*

5. The Blood and Sanctification

Hebrews 13 : 12 says.

"Therefore Jesus also, that He might sanctify the people with His own blood, suffered outside the gate."

The blood not only cleanses sin's record; it cleanses the conscience (Hebrews 9 : 14).

Authority requires purity; the conscience washed by the blood produces boldness in prayer.

> "The blood doesn't just forgive your past - it empowers your present."

6. The Blood and Access

Hebrews 10:19-22:

"Having boldness to enter the Holiest by the blood of Jesus..."

The veil of separation is gone. The believer no longer approaches God timidly but confidently.

The blood is our permanent **security clearance** into Heaven's throne room.

> "The blood opens every door between God and man."

7. The Blood and Protection

At Passover, the Israelites applied lamb's blood to their doorposts; judgment passed over them.

Exodus 12:13 records,

"When I see the blood, I will pass over you."

Today, the believer's life, home, and ministry are covered by the blood of the Lamb.

Satan's accusations cannot penetrate it.

Declaration: "I plead the blood of Jesus" is not superstition - it is *legal enforcement of covenant immunity.*

> "Where the blood is applied, destruction is denied."

8. The Blood and Authority Over Satan

Revelation 12:11 gives the strategy of victory:

"They overcame him by the blood of the Lamb and by the word of their testimony."

The blood breaks Satan's legal claim; testimony enforces the verdict.

Every time you declare the power of the blood, you remind Hell that its jurisdiction was revoked at Calvary.

> "Satan is allergic to the blood—he cannot stay where it is honored."

9. The Blood and The Believer's Witness
Communion is the continual proclamation of Christ's blood. **1 Corinthians 11:26** says,

"As often as you eat this bread and drink this cup, you proclaim the Lord's death till He comes."

When the Church celebrates communion, it rehearses authority—announcing to principalities that the covenant still stands.

10. The Voice of the Blood
Hebrews 12:24 speaks of *"the blood of sprinkling that speaks better things than that of Abel."*

Abel's blood cried for vengeance; Jesus' blood cries for mercy.

That voice still echoes in Heaven's courtroom, interceding for us.

> "Even when you are silent, the blood is still speaking."

11. Applying the Blood
Application is both spiritual and practical:

1. **By Faith:** Acknowledge the blood's power daily (Romans

3:25).
2. **By Confession:** Declare what the blood accomplishes (Revelation 12:11).
3. **By Obedience:** Live a life worthy of the covenant (Hebrews 10:29).
4. **By Communion:** Renew remembrance and alignment with His victory.

> "Faith applies what Calvary supplied."

12. Reflection and Discussion

1. Why must authority be rooted in the blood rather than emotion or effort?
2. How does understanding the covenant dimension of the blood change prayer life?
3. In what ways can believers practically "plead the blood" today?
4. How does communion serve as a declaration of authority?
5. What does it mean that the blood "speaks better things"?

13. Practical Ministry Exercise
Class Activation:

Invite students to lead a time of corporate declaration using scriptures on the blood.

Have them anoint symbolic "doorposts" (perhaps the classroom entrance) while proclaiming:

Prayer Declaration:
"Father, I thank You for the blood of Jesus.

THE AUTHORITY OF THE BELIEVER

Through that blood I have redemption, righteousness, and victory.
The blood speaks for me, covers me, and protects all that belongs to me.
By the blood of the Lamb and the word of my testimony,
I overcome every accusation of the enemy.
I walk in covenant authority - secured, cleansed, and empowered. Amen."

Chapter Summary

- The blood of Jesus is Heaven's legal foundation for all authority.
- It redeems, justifies, sanctifies, protects, and gives access.
- Satan's power is broken wherever the blood is applied and declared.
- The believer's testimony enforces what the blood has achieved.
- The blood still speaks interceding, defending, and empowering today.

Key Verse for Memorization
"In Him we have redemption through His blood, the forgiveness of sins, according to the riches of His grace."
Ephesians 1:7

CHAPTER 7 - AUTHORITY OVER SATAN AND DEMONS

"Behold, I give unto you authority to trample on serpents and scorpions, and over all the power of the enemy; and nothing shall by any means hurt you." Luke 10:19

Introduction — Understanding the Real Battle

Spiritual warfare is not a drama of equals. Satan is not God's rival; he is a created being already defeated at Calvary. Yet he continues to operate through ignorance, fear, and deception.

The believer's task is not to fight for victory but to **enforce** the victory already won by Christ.

> "The devil is not powerless — he is defeated. The difference is enforcement."

1. The Origin of Satan's Rebellion

Isaiah 14 and Ezekiel 28 reveal the fall of Lucifer. He was created as a covering cherub, anointed with beauty and music, but pride corrupted his heart.

He desired worship reserved for God alone: *"I will ascend... I will be like the Most High."* (Isaiah 14 : 13-14).

Because of rebellion, he was cast down - from the mountain of God to the realm of darkness.

Key Principle: *Rebellion was the first sin in Heaven and remains the enemy of authority on earth.*

2. Satan's Current Status

Satan is a defeated foe but not yet a destroyed one. Colossians 2:15 declares that Christ "disarmed principalities and powers."

He has been legally stripped of authority, yet he continues to influence those who believe his lies.

Legal vs. Vital Victory

- **Legal:** Christ already won.
- **Vital:** The believer must apply that victory daily.

> "Victory declared must become victory enforced."

3. The Hierarchy of Evil Spirits

Ephesians 6 : 12 lists four ranks of spiritual wickedness:

1. Principalities - territorial rulers.
2. Powers - administrators of darkness.
3. Rulers of the darkness of this age - influencers of culture and ideology.
4. Spiritual hosts of wickedness - demonic forces in the heavenly (realms).

Understanding structure prevents fear and teaches discernment.

Key Idea: *Hell is organized, but Heaven reigns.*

4. Christ's Victory Over Satan

Through death and resurrection, Jesus took back the keys of death and Hades (Revelation 1:18).

He triumphed openly and delegated that authority to His Body. Believers are not wrestling to win; they are executing an existing verdict.

> "The Cross was the devil's final court appearance."

5. The Believer's Authority Over the Enemy

Luke 10:19 and Mark 16:17-18 both authorize believers to cast out demons and trample on the enemy.

This is delegated power (*exousia*) that operates through relationship, not ritual.

Requirements for Effective Authority

- **Identity:** Know you are seated with Christ.
- **Purity:** Unconfessed sin undermines spiritual credibility.
- **Faith:** Authority is released through confident command.
- **Submission:** You must be under authority to exercise authority (James 4:7).

> "Submission to God makes resistance to Satan effective."

6. Understanding Demonic Activity

Demons seek to **deceive, defile,** and **dominate.**

Their primary weapons are lies, temptations, and oppression. They operate where invited through fear, sin, occult involvement, or ignorance.

Believers must differentiate between the flesh, psychological issues, and spiritual influence - always responding with discernment and compassion.

> "Authority without discernment creates error; discernment without authority produces fear."

7. The Believer's Armor

Ephesians 6:13-18 describes the armor of God - a spiritual uniform of authority:

- Belt of Truth → Integrity and identity.
- Breastplate of Righteousness → Confidence before God.
- Shoes of Peace → Stability in mission.
- Shield of Faith → Defense against fiery darts.
- Helmet of Salvation → Protection of the mind.
- Sword of the Spirit → The Word of God.

> "The armor is Christ Himself put on by faith."

8. Binding and Loosing

Matthew 18:18 teaches that whatever is bound on earth is bound in heaven.

This judicial authority allows believers to forbid the operation of evil and permit the will of God.

Example:

Binding fear, oppression, and division; loosing peace, healing, and unity.

Key Principle: *Binding is restriction; loosing is release.*

9. Deliverance Ministry

Deliverance is the application of Christ's authority to set captives free (Luke 4 : 18).

It is not a spectacle but a restoration of order. Believers must minister with love, purity, and wisdom.

Guidelines

1. Discern before acting.
2. Use the Name of Jesus only — not formulas.
3. Command, don't negotiate.
4. Maintain privacy and dignity of the person.
5. Follow up with discipleship and renewal of the mind.

> "Deliverance is not about shouting at demons but about restoring divine order in a soul."

10. Territorial Authority

Daniel 10 shows spiritual forces assigned to regions ("the prince of Persia").

The Church operates as God's embassy in each territory.

Through corporate prayer and proclamation, we break spiritual strongholds and release light into darkened cultures.

> "When the Church prays in unity, cities shift under the weight of Heaven's government."

11. Weapons of Victory

2 Corinthians 10:4 "The weapons of our warfare are not carnal but mighty through God."

Our arsenal includes the Word, the Name, the Blood, praise, fasting, and obedience.

These are not ceremonial acts but spiritual technologies that displace darkness.

> "Praise confuses hell; obedience disarms it."

12. Common Errors in Spiritual Warfare

1. **Fear-based warfare** - magnifying Satan instead of Christ.
2. **Formula warfare** - repetition without relationship.
3. **Arrogant warfare** - challenging principalities without instruction.
4. **Neglect of discipleship** - freedom without formation leads to return (Luke 11:24-26).

> "You cannot cast out what you continue to cultivate."

13. The Lifestyle of Authority

Authority is not an event but a lifestyle of communion, obedience, and humility.

Daily resistance (James 4:7) and constant filling with the Spirit (Ephesians 5:18) keep the believer victorious.

THE AUTHORITY OF THE BELIEVER

> "Authority grows in the soil of intimacy with God."

14. Reflection and Discussion

1. How does Christ's victory define our approach to spiritual warfare?
2. What are the dangers of pride or fear in dealing with demons?
3. Why is submission to authority essential for exercising authority?
4. How can churches establish territorial prayer strategies?
5. What balances power with wisdom in deliverance ministry?

15. Practical Ministry Exercise

Group Activation:

Lead students in a time of praise-based spiritual warfare. Have them declare Scriptures aloud such as Luke 10:19, Ephesians 6:10-18, and Romans 16:20.

Prayer Declaration:

"Father, thank You for Christ's victory.
In His Name I stand in authority over every work of darkness.
I am under Your authority and empowered by Your Spirit.
I bind confusion and loose peace; I bind fear and loose faith.
The enemy is beneath my feet.
I walk in boldness, purity, and victory through Jesus Christ. Amen."

Chapter Summary

- Satan was defeated through the Cross but must be resisted through faith.
- Authority flows from submission and identity in Christ.

- Discernment and compassion govern spiritual warfare.
- The weapons of the believer are spiritual and mighty through God.
- True victory is sustained by intimacy, humility, and obedience.

Key Verse for Memorization
"Therefore submit to God. Resist the devil and he will flee from you."
James 4:7

CHAPTER 8 - AUTHORITY IN PRAYER AND INTERCESSION

"Whatever you bind on earth will be bound in heaven, and whatever you loose on earth will be loosed in heaven." Matthew 18:18

Introduction - Prayer as Partnership, Not Persuasion

True prayer is not an attempt to convince a reluctant God to act, but an invitation for the believer to **enforce Heaven's will on earth.**

Prayer is the legislative function of the Kingdom - where sons and daughters of God execute divine decrees through their words, faith, and alignment with His Spirit.

When prayer flows from authority, it stops being begging and becomes **binding**; it stops being reaction and becomes **rule.**

> *"Prayer is not trying to get God to agree with us; it is agreeing with God to govern through us."*

1. The Legal Foundation of Prayer

Prayer is rooted in **covenant law**, not emotion.
God only obligates Himself to fulfill His *Word*.
Isaiah 43:26 says, *"Put Me in remembrance; let us contend together."*
He invites us to bring His Word as legal evidence.
Key Principle: *The believer who prays the Word never prays amiss.*

2. The Twofold Nature of Prayer

1. **Communion:** Fellowship with the Father - intimacy, worship, relationship.
2. **Legislation:** Exercising Kingdom authority - decrees, petitions, and enforcement.

Both are essential: intimacy gives revelation; revelation gives authority.

> "Authority without intimacy becomes mechanical; intimacy without authority becomes powerless."

3. Intercession Defined

Intercession means **standing in the gap** (Ezekiel 22:30) becoming a spiritual bridge between Heaven's will and earth's need.

It involves identification, compassion, and authority.

An intercessor is a priest who pleads and a warrior who decrees.

Illustration:

Moses stood between God and Israel (Exodus 32:11–14). His prayer altered national destiny.

> "Intercession is the courtroom where mercy overrules judgment."

4. The Priestly and Kingly Dimensions

Revelation 1:6 declares believers are *"kings and priests unto God."*

As priests we intercede; as kings we legislate.

Both functions operate through prayer: one releases compassion, the other commands completion.

Key Concept: *Priests plead from earth; kings decree from Heaven - but the believer does both.*

5. The Role of the Holy Spirit in Intercession

Romans 8:26–27 reveals that "the Spirit Himself makes intercession for us with groanings which cannot be uttered."

The Holy Spirit is the **Administrator of prayer.**
He interprets the mind of God and transmits it through the believer's spirit.
Praying in tongues activates this divine intercession beyond human knowledge.

> "When you pray in the Spirit, you stop informing God and start partnering with Him."

6. The Authority of Agreement
Jesus said in **Matthew 18:19**,

"If two of you agree on earth concerning anything they ask, it will be done."

The word *agree* (Greek *sumphōneō*) means "to harmonize like musical instruments."
Corporate prayer multiplies authority.
One can chase a thousand, but two can chase ten thousand (Deuteronomy 32:30).

> "Harmony in prayer creates symphonies of victory."

7. The Power of Binding and Loosing
Binding and loosing (Matthew 18:18) represent legal authorization.

- **Bind (deo)** - to forbid, restrain, declare unlawful.

- **Loose (luo)** - to release, permit, set free.

In prayer, believers forbid the operation of evil and release the purposes of God.
Binding is defense; loosing is offense.
Example:
Bind sickness, division, fear; loose healing, unity, and peace.

> "Binding limits darkness; loosing unlocks destiny."

8. The Watchman Anointing
<u>Isaiah 62:6 – 7</u>:

"I have set watchmen on your walls, O Jerusalem; they shall never hold their peace."

A **watchman** sees spiritually before others and sounds the alarm through prayer.

Intercessors carry prophetic sensitivity to detect what Heaven desires and what Hell attempts.

Key Principle: *Intercession is intelligence warfare in the Spirit.*

> "Watchmen don't predict the future—they protect it."

9. The Authority of Decree
<u>Job 22:28</u> says,

"You will also decree a thing, and it will be established for you."

Decrees are not requests; they are pronouncements based on divine law.

When spoken in faith, they carry Heaven's backing because they echo Heaven's will.

Illustration:
Elijah decreed the drought and rain (1 Kings 17 – 18).

His words controlled the climate because they aligned with Heaven's timing.

> "When your words agree with His Word, creation must comply."

10. Standing in the Gap for Nations

God seeks intercessors to stand for families, cities, and nations (Ezekiel 22 : 30).

Abraham interceded for Sodom (Genesis 18).

Daniel prayed for Israel's restoration (Daniel 9).

> "Nations rise and fall on the prayers of hidden intercessors."

National authority is exercised through prophetic intercession — the Church legislating righteousness over nations.

11. Hindrances to Authoritative Prayer

Hindrance	Description	Remedy
Unforgiveness	Blocks Heaven's flow (Mark 11:25)	Release and bless.
Doubt	Neutralizes decree (James 1:6–7)	Believe the Word.
Disobedience	Breaks alignment (1 John 3:22)	Obey promptly.
Ignorance	Lack of Word revelation	Study and confess truth.

> *"Unresolved offense silences authority."*

12. The Posture of Boldness

Hebrews 4:16 commands,

"Let us therefore come boldly to the throne of grace."

Boldness is not arrogance but covenant confidence.

It comes from righteousness consciousness and revelation of sonship.

God delights in confident sons, not timid servants.

> *"Fear prays for survival; faith prays for dominion."*

13. The Intercessor's Reward

God remembers intercessors.

Abraham became the father of nations; Job's captivity turned when he prayed for his friends; Anna's prayer prepared the coming of the Messiah.

Intercession writes history in secret.

> "Heaven records the prayers earth forgets."

14. Reflection and Discussion

1. How does authority change the way you define prayer?
2. What is the difference between supplication and legislation?
3. How does the Holy Spirit lead effective intercession?
4. Why is unity essential for corporate authority?
5. In what ways can you function as a watchman in your ministry or city?

15. Practical Ministry Exercise
Class Activation:
Divide students into prayer pairs or groups of three. Assign each team a theme: family, church, community, or nation.

Have them identify what to bind and what to loose according to Scripture, then pray bold, Word-based decrees together.

Prayer Declaration:
"Father, we align with Your will and speak Your Word in authority.
We bind confusion, darkness, and fear.
We loose peace, righteousness, and divine order.
As watchmen, we decree that Your Kingdom come and Your will be done.
We intercede with faith, legislate with power, and worship with confidence.
In Jesus' Name, amen."

Chapter Summary

- Prayer is partnership with God to enforce His will.
- Intercession is priestly compassion combined with kingly authority.

- The Holy Spirit empowers intercession beyond human knowledge.
- Agreement multiplies authority; decrees establish outcomes.
- Binding and loosing are legal operations of Heaven's Kingdom.
- Bold, Word-based, Spirit-led prayer governs outcomes on earth.

Key Verse for Memorization
"The effective, fervent prayer of a righteous man avails much."
James 5:16

CHAPTER 9 - AUTHORITY IN DAILY LIVING

"For if by the one man's offense death reigned through the one, much more those who receive abundance of grace and of the gift of righteousness will reign in life through the One, Jesus Christ." Romans 5:17

Introduction — The Practical Side of Dominion

Many Christians grasp spiritual authority in theory but live beneath it in practice.

Authority is not exercised only in miracles or warfare; it is revealed in how we manage thoughts, emotions, time, words, money, and relationships.

The same grace that enables us to cast out demons also enables us to *govern ourselves.*

1. The Call to Reign in Life

> "Before you rule nations, learn to rule your own nature."

Romans 5:17 teaches that believers "reign in life."

To reign means to *exercise dominion* - to bring every area of existence under divine order.

Authority is not about control but stewardship—governing life according to God's Word and character.

Key Idea:

The goal of redemption is restoration of rulership - life lived from the throne, not from reaction.

2. Authority Begins with Self-Government

Proverbs 16:32 says,
"He who rules his spirit is better than he who takes a city."

> *"Spiritual power without moral discipline is a weapon without safety."*

If you cannot rule *within*, you cannot rule *without*.

Self-control is the first proof of true authority.

The fruit of the Spirit (Galatians 5:22–23) are not decorations—they are the evidence of inner government.

3. Authority Over the Mind

The mind is the battlefield of dominion.

2 Corinthians 10:5 commands us to "take every thought captive."

To live victoriously, the believer must regulate imagination, reasoning, and perspective through the Word.

Steps to Mental Authority

1. **Renew the Mind** - Romans 12:2
2. **Guard the Input** - Philippians 4:8
3. **Reject Lies Quickly** - John 8:32
4. **Speak Truth Aloud** - Psalm 119:11

> *"Authority in prayer is maintained by purity in thought."*

4. Authority Over the Tongue

Proverbs 18:21: *"Death and life are in the power of the tongue."*

THE AUTHORITY OF THE BELIEVER

Our words create environments.

To live under divine authority, our speech must align with Heaven's vocabulary, truth, faith, and grace.

Practical Guidelines

- Replace complaint with confession of faith.
- Refuse gossip and slander.
- Speak blessing, not bitterness.
- Prophesy the Word over circumstances.

> "Your tongue is the steering wheel of your destiny."

5. Authority Over Emotions

Jesus modeled emotional mastery - He wept, yet never lost control.

Ephesians 4:26 says, *"Be angry, and do not sin."*

Feelings are real but not rulers. The believer must discern emotions without being driven by them.

Emotional Governance

- Submit emotions to the Spirit.
- Forgive quickly.
- Replace fear with faith.
- Rest instead of react.

> "Emotions are servants; never let them be kings."

6. Authority in Relationships

Authority does not mean domination; it means *servant leadership*.

In the home, workplace, and church, believers express dominion through humility, honor, and love.

Sphere **Expression of Authority**
Marriage Loving headship & mutual respect (Ephesians 5:21–33)
Parenting Training in Word & example (Proverbs 22:6)
Workplace Integrity & diligence (Colossians 3:23)
Church Submission to godly order (Hebrews 13:17)

> "True authority always protects; it never manipulates."

7. Financial Stewardship and Kingdom Economics

Authority includes dominion over resources.

Deuteronomy 8:18 reminds us: *"It is He who gives you power to get wealth."*

Finances are a test of trust. Tithing, giving, and generosity express submission to the King's economy.

Principles

1. God owns everything; we manage it.
2. Giving breaks greed's authority.
3. Faithfulness in little releases much.
4. Wealth with purpose advances the Gospel.

8. Authority in Time Management

Psalm 90:12 *"Teach us to number our days."*

Time is the currency of destiny.

Living under divine authority requires intentional stewardship of hours and seasons.

Practical Tools

- Plan prayer and rest intentionally.
- Prioritize eternal outcomes over urgent distractions.
- Align daily schedules with divine assignments.

> "Authority over time is mastery of purpose."

9. Authority in Speech and Witness
Daily dominion extends to testimony.
Matthew 5:16 *"Let your light so shine before men."*
Our conduct and words are Kingdom propaganda; integrity authenticates authority.

> "Your life is the loudest sermon you will ever preach."

10. Walking in Peace and Joy
Romans 14:17 *"The kingdom of God is righteousness and peace and joy in the Holy Spirit."*
Peace is not absence of conflict but presence of control. Joy is strength (Nehemiah 8:10).
Maintaining peace and joy in adversity proves dominion.

> "Storms reveal who truly reigns inside you."

11. The Culture of Honor
1 Peter 2:17 *"Honor all people."*

Honor recognizes God's image in others. It releases authority because dishonor blocks flow.

Jesus could not perform many miracles where He was dishonored (Mark 6:5).

12. Sustaining Authority Through Integrity

> "You can't receive from what you dishonor."

Proverbs 11:3 *"The integrity of the upright will guide them."*

Authority collapses when character cracks.
Private holiness preserves public power.

Integrity Checklist

- Be honest when unseen.
- Keep promises.
- Guard purity.
- Confess faults quickly.

> "Anointing impresses people; integrity keeps influence."

13. Daily Dominion Habits

1. Begin every morning with declaration of identity.
2. Feed daily on the Word.
3. Guard the gates - eyes, ears, mouth.
4. Walk in continual gratitude.

5. End each day with reflection and repentance.

> "Consistency turns revelation into lifestyle."

14. Reflection and Discussion

1. How does self-discipline relate to spiritual authority?
2. In what practical ways can you reign in life daily?
3. What area of personal life most challenges your dominion?
4. How do finances and time reveal submission to God?
5. Why is integrity the backbone of sustained authority?

15. Practical Ministry Exercise
Personal Assignment:

Ask each student to evaluate three personal areas where disorder still rules - thoughts, habits, or relationships.

Then write a daily dominion plan: one Scripture, one confession, one practical step for each.

Prayer Declaration:

"Father, thank You that I reign in life through Jesus Christ.

I bring every thought, word, and action under Your authority.

I rule my spirit with peace, my mind with truth, and my body with purity.

I will walk in integrity, steward time and treasure wisely, and display Your Kingdom daily.

Through me, may others see that Christ truly reigns. Amen."

Chapter Summary

- Authority is proven first in self-government.

- Dominion extends to thoughts, words, emotions, and stewardship.
- Daily habits manifest internal rulership.
- Peace, joy, and integrity demonstrate true Kingdom power.
- The believer's lifestyle preaches louder than any sermon.

Key Verse for Memorization
"The righteous shall live by faith." **Romans 1:17**

CHAPTER 10 - HEALING AND AUTHORITY

"He called His twelve disciples together, and gave them power and authority over all devils, and to cure diseases." Luke 9:1

Introduction — Healing: A Kingdom Mandate

Healing is not an optional ministry; it is part of the Gospel's core message.

Everywhere Jesus proclaimed the Kingdom, He also demonstrated it by healing the sick, cleansing lepers, and restoring the broken.

Sickness was never God's tool to humble His children; it was the devil's device to oppress them.

Christ's victory restored not only man's soul but his body and mind.

> "Healing is not a side benefit of redemption - it is part of salvation's covenant."

1. The Origin of Sickness

The fall of man opened the door for corruption, decay, and death. Before sin entered, there was no sickness, disease, or pain.

Romans 5:12 explains: *"Through one man sin entered the world, and death through sin."*

All sickness is the offspring of death - the product of separation from divine life.

Key Principle: *Sickness is not natural to redeemed humanity; it is a trespasser on covenant property.*

2. Christ's Victory Over Sickness

Isaiah 53:4-5 declares,

"Surely He has borne our griefs and carried our sorrows... and by His stripes we are healed."

The Hebrew words *choli* (sickness) and *makob* (pain) confirm that physical healing is included in the atonement.

At the whipping post, Jesus took our infirmities so that healing could be our inheritance.

Matthew 8:16–17 confirms Isaiah's prophecy was fulfilled in His ministry.

> "The Cross purchased forgiveness for the soul and healing for the body — both paid by the same blood."

3. The Believer's Right to Healing

Healing is not earned; it is received by faith in the finished work of Christ.

Just as salvation is accepted through faith, healing must also be *appropriated* through faith.

Mark 5:34 *"Daughter, your faith has made you well."*

Faith activates what grace has provided.

Authority enforces what faith receives.

> "Healing is God's provision; authority is the believer's enforcement."

4. The Ministry of Jesus as the Model

Jesus healed all who came to Him (Matthew 12 : 15). He never refused a single request for healing.

He revealed the Father's will through compassion and power. **Acts 10:38** summarizes His ministry:

"God anointed Jesus of Nazareth... who went about doing good and healing all who were oppressed by the devil."

Healing is the visible expression of divine compassion and the overthrow of Satanic oppression.

> "Every healing is Heaven declaring: The Kingdom has come."

5. The Delegation of Healing Authority

Luke 9:1-2 *"He gave them power and authority over all demons, and to cure diseases."*

This authority was later extended to the seventy disciples (Luke 10:9) and then to all believers (Mark 16:17-18).

The Church continues Jesus' healing ministry by acting in His Name and by His Spirit.

Key Concept: *We are not merely praying for healing; we are enforcing a covenant of health.*

6. Healing Through the Word

Psalm 107:20 says,

"He sent His word and healed them."

The Word of God carries healing virtue because it contains divine life.

When believed and spoken, the Word becomes medicine to the body (Proverbs 4 : 20-22).

> "The Word of God is the prescription; confession is the dosage."

7. Healing Through the Name of Jesus
Acts 3:6 "*In the name of Jesus Christ of Nazareth, rise up and walk.*"
The Name is the power of attorney for miracles.
When spoken in faith, it transfers the authority of Christ into the situation.
It's not the voice that heals but the Name behind the voice.

> "The Name of Jesus is the believer's signature on Heaven's healing decree."

8. Healing Through the Laying On of Hands
Mark 16:18 "*They shall lay hands on the sick, and they shall recover.*"
The laying on of hands is a point of contact that releases divine power through faith and obedience.
It connects the spiritual with the physical.

> "Hands become conduits when hearts carry faith."

9. Healing Through the Prayer of Faith
James 5:14–15:

"*The prayer of faith will save the sick, and the Lord will raise him up.*"

It is not the length of prayer that heals but the faith within it.

Authority in prayer comes from knowing the will of God — that healing is always His desire.

> "Faith does not beg; it commands in agreement with Heaven."

10. Healing Through Communion

At the Lord's Table, the broken bread symbolizes Christ's body, given for our healing.

1 Corinthians 11:29-30 implies that many are weak or sick because they fail to discern the Lord's body.

To receive communion in faith is to renew covenant health.

> "Every communion service is a healing service when discernment is present."

11. Healing and the Holy Spirit

Romans 8:11 "*The Spirit who raised Jesus from the dead will quicken your mortal bodies.*"

Healing is the Spirit's quickening power at work in physical cells. Miracles occur when faith agrees with the Spirit's flow.

> "The Word declares healing; the Spirit performs it."

12. Hindrances to Healing

Hindrance	Description	Solution
Unbelief	Doubt cancels reception.	Feed on the Word; meditate daily.
Unforgiveness	Blocks the flow of grace.	Release offense and forgive.
Fear	Focuses on symptoms instead of promises.	Replace fear with faith declarations.
Ignorance	Not knowing covenant rights.	Study and apply the Word on healing.

> *"The devil cannot steal what you continually confess."*

13. Walking in Divine Health

Healing is not the end goal - health is.

3 John 2: *"I pray that you may prosper and be in health, just as your soul prospers."*

Divine health comes by consistent Word life, prayer, obedience, and peace.

Living free from offense, anxiety, and disobedience keeps the door closed to sickness.

> *"It's better to walk in health than to seek healing."*

14. Reflection and Discussion

1. What is the difference between healing and divine health?
2. Why is the atonement the legal basis for healing?

THE AUTHORITY OF THE BELIEVER 93

3. How do faith and authority work together to manifest healing?
4. What practical steps keep believers walking in health daily?
5. How does the Church continue Jesus' healing ministry today?

15. Practical Ministry Exercise
Healing Workshop:
Have students form small groups to minister to one another using the principles of Scripture, the Name, and the laying on of hands.

Encourage testimonies of healing and faith declarations.

Prayer Declaration:
"Father, I thank You that healing is mine through the blood of Jesus.

By Your stripes I am healed, and sickness has no right to my body.

I enforce Your victory with the authority of the Name of Jesus.

Holy Spirit, quicken my body and restore every cell to perfect order.

I walk in divine health, wholeness, and covenant power — now and always. Amen."

Chapter Summary

- Healing is included in redemption and belongs to every believer.
- The believer enforces healing through the Word, the Name, the Blood, and the Spirit.
- Authority in healing flows from identity and obedience.
- Hindrances must be removed for healing to manifest.
- God's desire is not only to heal but to maintain His people in continual health.

Key Verse for Memorization
"By His stripes we are healed." **Isaiah 53:5**

CHAPTER 11 - AUTHORITY IN THE CHURCH

"And He put all things under His feet, and gave Him to be head over all things to the church, which is His body." Ephesians 1:22-23

Introduction - The Church: The Extension of Christ's Reign

The Church is not a religious institution; it is a divine organism; the visible expression of the invisible Christ.

Jesus is the Head; believers are His Body. Through His Church, He continues to rule, teach, heal, deliver, and demonstrate the Kingdom on earth.

Authority in the Church is not dictatorship but **delegated stewardship**; leadership that represents Heaven's government in humility and truth.

> "The Church is not a building filled with members; it is a Body filled with authority."

1. Christ, the Head of the Church
Colossians 1:18 says,
"He is the head of the body, the church."
All legitimate authority in the Church flows from Christ.
He governs through His Word and His Spirit, not through human ambition.
Every leader and believer functions only under His Lordship.
Key Principle: *Christ's authority is the source, not the supplement, of Church leadership.*

> "No man truly leads in the Church until he first follows Christ."

2. The Church as His Body

1 Corinthians 12 describes believers as many members forming one body.

Each member has unique gifts and functions, but all operate under one Head.

The hand cannot dominate the eye, nor the foot despise the ear.

Unity, not uniformity, is the power of the Body.

Disorder in the Body weakens authority; alignment strengthens it.

> "Authority in the Body flows through alignment with the Head."

3. Spiritual Government in the Church

Ephesians 4:11–12 outlines the fivefold ministry: apostles, prophets, evangelists, pastors, and teachers.

These are not titles of superiority but functions of responsibility.

Their purpose is "for the equipping of the saints... for the edifying of the body of Christ."

Authority in Church leadership is **functional** (for service), not **positional** (for control).

Ministry Office	Function	Authority Expression
Apostle	Foundation & order	Visionary authority
Prophet	Revelation & direction	Spiritual discernment
Evangelist	Expansion	Evangelistic authority
Pastor	Care & guidance	Relational authority
Teacher	Doctrine & clarity	Instructional authority

> "In the Church, authority is not rank; it is responsibility."

4. The Authority of the Local Church

Every local congregation is a micro-embassy of Heaven.

Jesus said, *"Where two or three are gathered in My name, there am I in the midst of them."* (Matthew 18:20).

The Church carries collective authority to bind and loose, to discipline and restore, to pray and govern.

Key Idea: *The local church is God's authorized agency for spiritual order in the community.*

> "Cities are transformed when churches understand their jurisdiction."

5. Authority Through Unity

Psalm 133 declares that where brethren dwell in unity, the Lord commands blessing.

Disunity is Hell's oldest strategy to weaken the Church's influence.

Unity multiplies spiritual power because authority flows through agreement.

Illustration:

In Acts 2, they were "in one accord," and the Spirit fell. In Acts 4, they prayed "with one voice," and the place shook.

> *"Agreement is the amplifier of authority."*

6. Authority in Worship

Worship is not entertainment; it is **enthronement.**

Psalm 22:3 says, *"God inhabits the praises of His people."*

When the Church worships in Spirit and truth, God's throne becomes manifest among His people, and demonic oppression is displaced.

> *"Every time the Church truly worships, Heaven establishes a throne on earth."*

7. Authority in Teaching and Doctrine

Sound doctrine preserves spiritual authority.

Titus 2:1 *"Speak the things which are proper for sound doctrine."*

False teaching weakens faith and distorts authority.

The Church must guard truth with love and teach the Word without compromise.

> *"Authority is sustained by truth and destroyed by error."*

8. Authority in Discipline and Correction

Matthew 18:15–17 and 1 Corinthians 5 teach that church discipline is necessary to maintain purity and order.

Correction is not cruelty - it is covenant love.

Unchecked sin invites confusion and loss of credibility.

Key Principle: *Restoration, not humiliation, is the goal of correction.*

> *"Authority without accountability becomes abuse; accountability without grace becomes legalism."*

9. The Role of Submission

Hebrews 13:17 commands believers to "obey those who rule over you and be submissive, for they watch for your souls."

Submission is not slavery; it is voluntary cooperation with divine order.

Rebellion fractures anointing; submission multiplies it.

> *"Submission is the soil where authority grows."*

10. The Authority of Corporate Prayer

When believers pray in agreement, the Church legislates spiritual realities.

Acts 12 records that Peter's imprisonment was overturned by united prayer.

Corporate intercession carries governmental weight because it represents the Body speaking with one voice.

> "When the Church prays as one, Heaven moves as one."

11. The Authority of Love

Love is the greatest power in the Church.
Galatians 5:6 declares that "faith works by love."
Without love, authority becomes tyranny.
Love turns leadership into service and power into grace.

> "The measure of true authority is how well one serves."

12. The Authority of the Anointing

Isaiah 10:27 "The anointing breaks the yoke."

In the Church, every member carries a measure of anointing to serve, edify, and build others.

When believers operate in their anointing under order, the Church functions with supernatural power.

> "Organization gives structure; anointing gives life."

13. Dangers to Authority in the Church

Danger	Effect	Remedy
Pride	Corrupts leadership	Cultivate humility
Division	Weakens power	Walk in unity
Doctrinal Error	Breeds deception	Return to Scripture
Abuse of Power	Wounds believers	Restore servant heart
Neglect of Prayer	Drains anointing	Return to intimacy

> "Where prayer ceases, authority leaks."

14. The Church as a Governing Ekklesia

The Greek word for Church, *ekklesia,* means "called-out assembly" - a legislative body that represents the King's will.

The early Church saw itself as Heaven's parliament on earth.

Through preaching, prayer, and proclamation, it released Heaven's decrees over nations.

> "The Church is not a crowd of spectators but a council of governors."

15. Reflection and Discussion

1. How does Christ's headship define leadership in the Church?
2. What is the difference between authority and control?
3. How can unity and sound doctrine preserve spiritual power?
4. Why is submission essential for order and blessing?
5. What does it mean to see the Church as an *ekklesia* rather than just a congregation?

16. Practical Ministry Exercise
Group Activation:

Have students design a model of spiritual order for a local church (leadership roles, intercessory teams, outreach).

Include Scriptures defining how authority flows from Christ through His people.

Prayer Declaration:
"Lord Jesus, You are the Head of the Church.
We submit to Your authority and align with Your order.
Let Your will govern our worship, teaching, and service.
Empower leaders with humility and members with unity.
Make Your Church a throne of Your glory on earth.
We decree: Your Kingdom come, Your will be done in Your Body. Amen."

Chapter Summary

- Christ is the Head; the Church is His Body.
- All Church authority flows from His Lordship and Word.
- Spiritual government is servanthood, not domination.
- Unity, love, and sound doctrine sustain power.
- The Church functions as Heaven's governing council on earth.

Key Verse for Memorization

"Upon this rock I will build My church, and the gates of hell shall not prevail against it."
Matthew 16:18

CHAPTER 12 - AUTHORITY IN THE NAME OF JESUS - REVISITED AND PRACTICALLY APPLIED

"At the name of Jesus every knee should bow, of those in heaven, and of those on earth, and of those under the earth." Philippians 2:10

Introduction - From Revelation to Operation

In earlier chapters we discovered that the Name of Jesus embodies His person, His power, and His presence.

Yet revelation without application remains unfruitful. This chapter transitions from **understanding** the Name to **using** it effectively - in prayer, ministry, and daily dominion.

> *"Revelation of the Name gives confidence; application of the Name brings conquest."*

1. The Legal Power Behind the Name

When Jesus declared, *"All authority in heaven and on earth has been given to Me"* (Matthew 28:18), He was announcing a transfer of jurisdiction.

Believers act **in His stead**, representing Him legally in the earth.

This is not metaphorical - it is the divine charter of the Church's operation.

Key Idea:

The Name of Jesus is Heaven's signature on earth's decrees.

> *"Using His Name is not reciting syllables; it is executing a covenant."*

2. The Principle of Representation
John 14:13 *"Whatever you ask in My name, that I will do."*
In ancient law, a representative carried a *seal* of authority.

To act *in the name of* another meant your actions were legally binding on their behalf.

When the believer acts in the Name of Jesus, it is as though **Jesus Himself were present and acting.**

Illustration:

A police officer's badge does not make him powerful; the government backing the badge does.

Likewise, the believer's words in the Name carry the weight of Heaven's government.

3. Using the Name in Prayer
The Pattern:

1. **Ask the Father** - our petitions are directed to God (John 16:23).
2. **In the Name of Jesus** - our access and authority rest in Christ's merit.
3. **In Faith** - confidence that it is already granted (Mark 11:24).

When you pray "in Jesus' Name," you are not closing a prayer - you are **opening a decree.**

> *"Prayer in the Name of Jesus is Heaven's language of authorization."*

4. Using the Name in Healing and Deliverance

The apostles never healed in their own strength but always **in His Name**.

Acts 3:6 "*In the name of Jesus Christ of Nazareth, rise up and walk.*"
Acts 16:18 "*I command you in the name of Jesus Christ to come out.*"
The Name is the believer's spiritual badge.

Sickness, demons, and fear must submit when the command is issued in faith.

> *"The enemy recognizes the Name only when it is spoken by revelation, not repetition."*

5. Using the Name in Evangelism

Mark 16:17-18 "*In My name they will cast out demons… they will lay hands on the sick.*"

The proclamation of the Gospel is incomplete without demonstration.

When the Name is declared publicly, it confronts darkness with the evidence of resurrection power.

Illustration:

In the book of Acts, the early Church didn't debate demonic powers; they displaced them.

> "Evangelism without authority is information; evangelism with His Name is transformation."

6. The Name and Spiritual Warfare

Philippians 2:9–10 reveals that Jesus' Name is exalted above all names.

Every demonic power, curse, or principality must bow to it.

When facing spiritual opposition, believers do not plead for deliverance - they *declare* the Name as final jurisdiction.

Practical Step:
Speak the Word aloud and then seal it with the Name.
"It is written... in the Name of Jesus!"

> "The Word declares the verdict; the Name enforces it."

7. The Name and Daily Dominion

Colossians 3:17 *"Whatever you do in word or deed, do all in the name of the Lord Jesus."*

Authority in the Name is not limited to church services - it covers daily life.

You face temptation, fear, or pressure by declaring your position:
"In the Name of Jesus, I have peace."
"In the Name of Jesus, anxiety must leave."
"In the Name of Jesus, this situation will align with God's Word."

> "The Name of Jesus is not only for casting out demons but for conquering daily life."

8. The Power of Confession

The spoken word releases the power of the Name.

Revelation 12:11 *"They overcame him by the blood of the Lamb and by the word of their testimony."*

When believers continually confess the authority of the Name, they maintain spiritual territory.

Daily Confession Example

"In Jesus' Name, I am victorious.

In Jesus' Name, fear and sickness bow.

In Jesus' Name, my home is protected.

In Jesus' Name, the Kingdom of God advances through me."

> "The more you confess the Name, the more your reality conforms to its power."

9. The Name and the Holy Spirit

The Holy Spirit confirms and manifests whatever is done in the Name of Jesus.

John 16:14 *"He will glorify Me, for He will take of what is Mine and declare it to you."*

The Spirit and the Name operate inseparably.

Whenever you act in the Name, the Spirit moves to fulfill it.

10. The Name and Worship

> "The Spirit executes what the Name authorizes."

Worship exalts the Name above all else.

Philippians 2:10 *every knee bows at that Name.*

When the Church magnifies Jesus, His authority fills the atmosphere.

Worship becomes warfare; praise becomes proclamation.

> "When you lift the Name, the throne descends."

11. The Misuse of the Name

Acts 19:13–16 records sons of Sceva using the Name without relationship.

They had formula but no faith.

The Name cannot be used mechanically; it requires revelation, righteousness, and relationship.

> "You cannot use the Name of Jesus against a devil you fellowship with."

12. Developing Confidence in the Name

Confidence grows through:

1. **Revelation** - meditate on Scriptures about His authority.
2. **Application** - use the Name consistently.
3. **Testimony** - recall answered prayers and victories.
4. **Holiness** - walk in purity, which preserves authority.

Key Principle: *Authority unused becomes authority forgotten.*

13. Reflection and Discussion

1. Why is the Name of Jesus more than a closing phrase in prayer?
2. How does revelation affect the effectiveness of the Name?
3. What safeguards prevent misuse of the Name?
4. How can believers apply the Name in daily life situations?
5. Why is the Name central to every aspect of ministry?

14. Practical Ministry Exercise

Group Practice:

Divide students into small teams to role-play different ministry situations - healing, intercession, deliverance, daily challenge.

Each team demonstrates how to apply the Name with Scripture and faith.

Prayer Declaration:

"Father, thank You for the authority of the Name of Jesus.

I declare that His Name is above all names, in Heaven and on earth.

I speak that Name over sickness, fear, and circumstance.

Every knee must bow and every tongue confess that Jesus Christ is Lord.

I walk daily in the power, peace, and presence of that Name. Amen."

Chapter Summary

- The Name of Jesus carries Heaven's legal and spiritual power.
- Believers act as Christ's representatives in His Name.
- The Name must be used with revelation, faith, and obedience.
- Prayer, healing, deliverance, and daily life all operate through the Name.
- The Spirit confirms what the Name authorizes.

Key Verse for Memorization

"Whatever you ask in My name, that I will do, that the Father may be glorified in the Son."
John 14:13

CHAPTER 13 - AUTHORITY OVER CIRCUMSTANCES AND THE NATURAL REALM

"Then He arose and rebuked the wind and the sea, and there was a great calm." Matthew 8:26

Introduction - Dominion Beyond the Invisible

Jesus demonstrated authority not only over demons but also over storms, hunger, lack, and even death.

He ruled both the **spiritual** and the **physical** because both were created by the same Word.

The believer, united with Christ, carries that same delegated dominion.

Faith makes the unseen Word govern the seen world.

> "Circumstances are temporary; authority is eternal."

1. The Dominion Mandate Restored

Genesis 1:26 *"Let them have dominion over the earth."*

The original design placed man as Heaven's steward over the material realm.

Sin fractured that rule, but redemption through Christ restored it (Psalm 8:6).

Believers are again called to subdue, not people, but problems, systems, and situations contrary to God's purpose.

Key Principle: *Redemption reinstates responsibility; authority restores stewardship.*

2. Jesus' Mastery over Nature

The Gospels record multiple instances where Jesus demonstrated physical dominion:

Event	Scripture	Lesson
Calming the storm	Matt 8:26	Peace commands chaos.
Feeding the 5,000	John 6:1-14	Provision multiplies under blessing.
Walking on water	Matt 14:25	Faith transcends natural law.
Withering the fig tree	Mark 11:14	Words carry governing power.

> *"Creation still recognizes the voice of its Creator — and that voice now speaks through you."*

3. The Word as the Governing Law

Hebrews 1:3 says that Christ upholds "all things by the word of His power."

The universe is word-controlled; therefore, words of faith can redirect outcomes.

Authority operates through spoken decree aligned with Scripture.

Illustration:

Just as a conductor's baton guides an orchestra, the believer's words guide the rhythm of circumstances.

> *"You cannot dominate circumstances you continue to describe."*

4. Authority over the Elements
Mark 4:39 *"Peace, be still!"*

Jesus rebuked the storm as if it were a rebellious spirit, and creation obeyed.

Nature responds to divine authority because it was birthed from divine speech.

Believers may likewise speak peace into literal storms, accidents, or crises.

Key Idea: *Faith does not deny natural reality; it imposes spiritual reality upon it.*

5. Authority over Lack and Provision

Luke 5:5-6 shows Peter's empty nets filled after obeying Jesus' word.

Kingdom authority includes provision; scarcity must yield to obedience.

The believer decrees alignment with covenant supply (Philippians 4:19).

> "Provision is not luck; it is the natural response to supernatural order."

6. Authority over Time and Seasons

Joshua 10:12-13 the *sun stood still.*

Time itself bowed to a man operating under divine command.

While we do not command celestial bodies, we can redeem time (Ephesians 5 : 16) through prayer, focus, and prophetic acceleration.

7. Authority in Crisis

When Paul was shipwrecked (Acts 27), his confidence preserved every life aboard.

Authority does not always remove storms; sometimes it governs outcomes within them.

Faith's peace transforms chaos into testimony.

Key Principle: *Authority speaks calm before the storm ends.*

8. Authority over Death and Disease

John 11:43 *"Lazarus, come forth!"*

Death obeyed the Word because it heard the Creator's voice through human lips.

That same resurrection authority operates in every Spirit-filled believer (Romans 8:11).

9. Faith as the Bridge Between Realms

> "Faith transfers divine intention into earthly manifestation."

Mark 11:23 *"Whoever says... and does not doubt in his heart... will have whatever he says."*

Faith is Heaven's transportation system — moving truth from the invisible into manifestation.

Authority without faith is law without enforcement.

10. Walking in Dominion Mindset

> "Your mind is either your mission control or your battlefield."

Romans 12:2 transformation begins by renewing the mind.

Believers must replace survival thinking with stewardship thinking.

Instead of asking "Why is this happening?" ask "What has Heaven authorized me to change?"

11. The Law of Commanded Blessing

Job 22:28 *"You will decree a thing, and it will be established for you."*

Commanded blessing manifests where alignment, faith, and obedience converge.

Circumstances may resist, but persistence in decree prevails.

> *"What you continually decree, you eventually see."*

12. Balancing Faith and Wisdom

Authority is never recklessness.

Jesus refused to jump from the temple (Matthew 4:7) proof that presumption is not faith.

We act only on the revealed Word and prompting of the Spirit.

> *"True faith never tempts God; it trusts Him."*

13. Reflection and Discussion

1. How does Christ's dominion extend into natural creation?
2. What distinguishes faith from presumption when commanding circumstances?
3. In what areas of life can you begin exercising redemptive authority?
4. Why is speech critical to enforcing authority over the natural?
5. How can believers steward power without pride or misuse?

14. Practical Ministry Exercise

Assignment:

Invite students to identify one real-life situation that appears unchangeable; a financial need, health issue, or family challenge.

Using Scripture, write a decree beginning with "It is written..." and ending with "In the Name of Jesus."

Read these aloud together as prophetic enforcement.

THE AUTHORITY OF THE BELIEVER

Prayer Declaration:
"Father, You gave us dominion through Christ.
We speak peace to storms, supply to lack, and order to confusion.
Circumstances bow to Your Word and obey the authority of Jesus' Name.
We reign in life through Him, establishing Heaven's order in every realm. Amen."

Chapter Summary

- Dominion covers both spiritual and natural realms.
- Words of faith govern circumstances just as God's Word governs creation.
- Lack, storms, and crises respond to divine decree.
- Faith is the bridge that brings invisible truth into visible order.
- Authority must be balanced by wisdom, humility, and continual dependence on God.

Key Verse for Memorization

"Whatever you bind on earth will be bound in heaven, and whatever you loose on earth will be loosed in heaven."
Matthew 18:18

CHAPTER 14
AUTHORITY IN THE HOLY SPIRIT AND SPIRITUAL GIFTS

"You shall receive power when the Holy Spirit has come upon you; and you shall be witnesses to Me." Acts 1:8

Introduction — The Administrator of Divine Authority

All authority flows from the Father, is granted through the Son, and is **administered by the Holy Spirit.**

Without the Spirit, revelation remains theory and authority remains dormant.

The Holy Spirit is the enforcer of the believer's dominion - the One who activates gifts, empowers service, and manifests Heaven's power on earth.

> *"The Holy Spirit is not a feeling to experience but a Person who empowers."*

1. The Holy Spirit — Heaven's Resident Power

Genesis 1:2 *"The Spirit of God was hovering over the face of the waters."*

From creation to Pentecost, the Spirit has been the executive power of God's Word.

He brings to life whatever the Word declares.

Key Principle: *The Father wills it, the Word speaks it, the Spirit performs it.*

> *"Where the Word is spoken in faith, the Spirit moves in power."*

2. The Promise of Power

THE AUTHORITY OF THE BELIEVER

Jesus commanded His disciples to wait in Jerusalem for the promise of the Father (Acts 1:4–8).

The baptism of the Holy Spirit is the empowerment for Kingdom representation.

Before Pentecost, they were called; after Pentecost, they were commissioned.

Illustration:

Before the Spirit came, Peter denied Christ; after, he declared Him before thousands.

> "The Holy Spirit turns believers into witnesses and witnesses into warriors."

3. The Spirit as the Enforcer of Authority

Romans 8:11 "The Spirit who raised Jesus from the dead will quicken your mortal bodies."

The same power that raised Christ resides in the believer.

Authority without the Spirit is lifeless law; with the Spirit, it becomes living force.

Key Idea: *The Holy Spirit is the Executor of Christ's authority on earth.*

> "When the Spirit moves, authority manifests."

4. The Spirit's Role in Revealing the Word

John 16:13 *"He will guide you into all truth."*

Revelation is the foundation of authority. The Spirit illuminates Scripture until it becomes personal truth, empowering action.

Without illumination, knowledge remains intellectual; with it, knowledge becomes transformational.

> "The Spirit does not add to Scripture; He activates it."

5. The Spirit and the Anointing

Isaiah 61:1 *"The Spirit of the Lord is upon Me, because He has anointed Me."*

The anointing is the manifestation of the Spirit's authority.

It breaks yokes (Isaiah 10:27) and destroys resistance.

Every believer carries a measure of this anointing to fulfill divine assignment.

> "The anointing is Heaven's endorsement on earthly obedience."

6. Spiritual Gifts — The Expression of Authority

1 Corinthians 12:7 *"The manifestation of the Spirit is given to each one for the profit of all."*

Spiritual gifts are tools of divine authority distributed for ministry effectiveness.

Each gift is a channel through which Christ continues His works through the Church.

Gift	Expression of Authority	Reference
Word of Wisdom	Governs direction	1 Cor. 12 : 8
Word of Knowledge	Reveals information	1 Cor. 12 : 8
Faith	Governs impossibilities	1 Cor. 12 : 9
Gifts of Healing	Governs sickness	1 Cor. 12 : 9
Working of Miracles	Governs nature	1 Cor. 12 : 10
Prophecy	Governs utterance	1 Cor. 12 : 10
Discerning of Spirits	Governs discernment	1 Cor. 12 : 10
Tongues & Interpretation	Governs communication	1 Cor. 12 : 10

> "The gifts of the Spirit are not decorations; they are instruments of dominion."

7. The Spirit's Partnership in Ministry

The early Church was led by the Spirit in every decision, appointments, journeys, and miracles.

Acts 13:2 "The Holy Spirit said, 'Separate unto Me Barnabas and Saul.'"

Authority in ministry flows from partnership, not performance.

Key Principle: *The Spirit leads; authority follows.*

> "We command with confidence only when we follow with obedience."

8. The Spirit of Boldness

Acts 4:31 "*They were all filled with the Holy Spirit, and they spoke the word of God with boldness.*"

Boldness is the mark of divine authority.

Timidity quenches the Spirit; confidence releases Him.

9. The Spirit of Wisdom and Counsel

Isaiah 11:2 describes the sevenfold Spirit of God: wisdom, understanding, counsel, might, knowledge, fear of the Lord.

This is divine intelligence that governs leadership decisions.

Authority must always be accompanied by wisdom to ensure righteous application.

> "Power without wisdom is dangerous; wisdom without power is limited."

10. The *Spirit's Role in Unity*

<u>Ephesians 4:3</u> *"Endeavor to keep the unity of the Spirit in the bond of peace."*

Authority functions through unity.

Division grieves the Spirit; harmony multiplies power.

The same Spirit that empowers also unites.

> "The Spirit who gives gifts also gives grace to work together."

11. The Spirit and Spiritual Warfare

Ephesians 6:17–18 connects the Word, prayer, and Spirit in battle.

The "sword of the Spirit" is the spoken Word, *rhema*, applied with authority.

Praying "in the Spirit" (Jude 20) builds spiritual stamina and sensitivity to God's strategy.

> "The Spirit supplies the strategy; the believer enforces the victory."

12. Flowing in the Gifts Responsibly

Authority in gifts must always submit to the order of love (1 Corinthians 13).

The Spirit never contradicts Scripture, glorifies man, or causes confusion.

Authentic manifestations magnify Jesus and edify His Body.

> "Love is the law that governs all power."

13. Revival and the Authority of the Spirit

Every revival in history has been a rediscovery of the Holy Spirit's authority.

When the Spirit is honored, miracles multiply, conviction deepens, and society transforms.

The Church's greatest need is not more programs but more power.

14. Reflection and Discussion

1. Why is the Holy Spirit essential for authority to operate effectively?
2. How do spiritual gifts express divine dominion?
3. What safeguards ensure that power is exercised responsibly?
4. How can believers maintain sensitivity to the Spirit's direction in ministry?
5. Why does love remain the foundation for all spiritual operation?

15. Practical Ministry Exercise
Activation Workshop:
Students gather for a session of prayer and worship focused on surrendering to the Holy Spirit.

Each student prays in the Spirit and listens for promptings.

Encourage operation in gifts such as prophecy, word of knowledge, or healing under pastoral supervision.

Prayer Declaration:
"Holy Spirit, I yield to You as the enforcer of Heaven's power.

Flow through me in wisdom, love, and strength.

Stir the gifts within me and confirm Your Word with signs following.

Let my authority be pure, humble, and Spirit-led. For Your glory alone. Amen."

Chapter Summary

- The Holy Spirit is the administrator of Christ's authority on earth.
- The baptism in the Spirit empowers believers for effective ministry.
- Spiritual gifts are expressions of divine dominion.
- Love, wisdom, and unity safeguard supernatural operation.
- The Church advances as it honors and partners with the Holy Spirit.

Key Verse for Memorization
"Not by might, nor by power, but by My Spirit, says the Lord of hosts."
Zechariah 4:6

CHAPTER 15 - MAINTAINING AUTHORITY THROUGH HOLINESS AND OBEDIENCE

"Behold, to obey is better than sacrifice, and to heed than the fat of rams."
1 Samuel 15:22

Introduction — Power Without Purity is Power at Risk
Authority is not only granted; it must be **guarded.**
Sin, pride, and disobedience weaken spiritual influence, even when the calling remains.
Holiness keeps authority *clean*, and obedience keeps it *current*.
Without these two virtues, even the most anointed vessel can lose effectiveness.

> *"Anointing may attract power, but holiness sustains it."*

1. The Connection Between Authority and Character
Luke 10:19 gives authority over serpents and scorpions, yet **Luke 10:20** reminds,

> *"Do not rejoice that spirits are subject to you, but that your names are written in heaven."*

Character matters more than performance.
Authority flows from identity, not emotion. Holiness preserves that identity before God.
Key Principle: *Private purity protects public power.*

> "A clean heart is Heaven's platform for authority."

2. Obedience — The Foundation of Spiritual Authority

Authority in the Kingdom is built upon **submission.**

Jesus, though the Son of God, learned obedience through what He suffered (Hebrews 5:8).

If even Christ's authority was perfected through obedience, so must ours.

Illustration:

Saul lost his kingdom, not because he was talentless, but because he was disobedient (1 Samuel 15).

Disobedience dethrones authority.

> "You cannot rule what you refuse to obey God about."

3. Holiness — The Atmosphere of Power

Holiness is not perfectionism; it is separation unto God.

It means being **different for a purpose**—set apart to represent His nature.

2 Timothy 2 : 21 *"If anyone cleanses himself, he will be a vessel for honor, sanctified and useful to the Master."*

> "Holiness is not bondage; it is the boundary that preserves freedom."

4. The Danger of Unchecked Sin

Sin dulls spiritual sensitivity and blocks divine flow.

Samson's strength remained until compromise became lifestyle. Delilah didn't cut his hair - disobedience did.

Key Lesson: *Authority cannot operate where compromise is tolerated.*

> "When sin enters, authority exits quietly."

5. Integrity — The Hidden Pillar of Power

Integrity means wholeness; being the same in secret as in public.

Psalm 15:1–2 describes those who "walk uprightly, work righteousness, and speak the truth in their heart."

Authority without integrity breeds corruption; integrity sustains credibility.

> "Integrity is what you keep when no one is watching."

6. Obedience as Worship

Obedience is not merely compliance; it is the highest form of worship.

Jesus said in **John 14:15**, *"If you love Me, keep My commandments."*

The true proof of love for God is not emotion, but submission.

Every act of obedience invites a greater measure of authority.

7. Consecration — Maintaining a Life Separated unto God

Romans 12:1 *"Present your bodies as a living sacrifice."*

Consecration is not a one-time event; it is a daily renewal of surrender.

Power leaks where consecration fades.

8. The Discipline of Prayer and the Word

Authority weakens when devotion is neglected.

Jesus maintained constant fellowship with the Father - that was the secret of His authority.

Prayer keeps alignment; the Word keeps clarity.

Practical Principle:
No Word, no weight; no prayer, no power.

> "The Word renews authority; prayer releases it."

9. Submission to Spiritual Authority

Holiness includes respecting divine order.

Hebrews 13:17 *"Obey those who rule over you... for they watch out for your souls."*

Submission is not humiliation but protection.

Rebellion forfeits covering and drains strength.

> "The mantle you honor is the mantle you inherit."

10. The Role of Repentance

> "Repentance does not reduce you — it renews you."

Repentance is the maintenance tool of authority.

It cleanses the conscience, restores alignment, and reopens the channel for divine flow.

Psalm 51 shows David's authority restored after failure through deep repentance.

11. Authority and Humility

James 4:6 *"God resists the proud but gives grace to the humble."*
Pride is authority's greatest enemy.
Humility acknowledges dependence on God; it keeps power safe within grace.

12. Walking in the Fear of the Lord

The fear of the Lord is not terror but reverence that produces obedience.

It keeps motives pure and decisions righteous.

Proverbs 8:13 *"The fear of the Lord is to hate evil."*

> "Authority is safe only in the hands of those who fear God."

13. Endurance in Testing

Authority is proven, not in comfort, but in testing.
Joseph's authority in Egypt was forged in the prison of obedience.
Every test you pass increases your trustworthiness before Heaven.

> "God promotes those who stay faithful when unseen."

14. Reflection and Discussion

1. Why must holiness and obedience be continual rather than occasional?
2. How does sin erode spiritual authority even when gifts remain?
3. What are practical ways to maintain purity in modern ministry?
4. Why does humility act as protection for spiritual power?
5. How does repentance renew authority in a believer's life?

15. Practical Ministry Exercise
Personal Consecration Assignment:
Have students spend a day in fasting and reflection, writing out any area of compromise or neglect that could hinder authority.

They will then pray Psalm 51 aloud and declare renewed dedication to holiness and obedience.

Prayer Declaration:
"Father, I consecrate myself anew to You.
Purify my motives, cleanse my heart, and align my will with Yours.
Let obedience become my delight, and holiness my lifestyle.
Keep me faithful, humble, and sensitive to Your Spirit.
May Your authority flow through a clean vessel for Your glory. Amen."

Chapter Summary

- Authority is sustained by holiness, obedience, and humility.
- Sin and pride silently erode spiritual influence.
- Integrity and consecration preserve credibility.
- Repentance restores power; obedience multiplies it.
- A holy life is the foundation of enduring authority.

Key Verse for Memorization
"Be holy, for I am holy." **1 Peter 1:16**

CHAPTER 16 - AUTHORITY IN THE END-TIME CHURCH

"Arise, shine; for your light has come! And the glory of the Lord is risen upon you." Isaiah 60:1

Introduction — The Church Triumphant, Not Terrified

The last days will not be defined by the triumph of darkness but by the *manifestation of the glorious Church*.

While the world staggers in fear, the Church will stand in **revelation, authority, and power.**

The same authority Christ gave His early disciples will be intensified in His end-time Body - purified through persecution, perfected in unity, and empowered by glory.

1. Prophetic Foundations for End-Time Authority

> "The end-time Church will not escape the world — it will transform it."

Jesus declared, *"This gospel of the kingdom shall be preached in all the world as a witness to all nations, and then the end will come."* **Matthew 24 : 14**

End-time authority is evangelistic, apostolic, and supernatural.

Before Christ's return, the Church must demonstrate the Kingdom, not merely discuss it.

> "The first Church was born in fire; the last Church will finish in glory."

Key Principle: *The final move of God will restore the original mandate; dominion through discipleship.*

2. The Rise of the Glorious Church

Ephesians 5:27 says Christ will present to Himself *"a glorious Church, not having spot or wrinkle."*

This speaks of purity and maturity.

Authority in the end-time Church will not rest on titles or structures, but on *consecrated character and spiritual stature.*

> "Power without purity will have no platform in the last days."

3. Increased Darkness, Greater Light

Isaiah 60:2 *"Darkness shall cover the earth... but the Lord will arise over you."*

Authority shines brightest amid crisis.

Economic turmoil, political unrest, and moral confusion will only create the stage for God's sons to manifest dominion.

Illustration:

In Egypt, while plagues spread, light remained in Goshen (Exodus 10:23).

The end-time Church will be the *Goshen of grace* - untouchable, radiant, and redemptive.

> "The darker the night, the brighter the authority of light."

4. The Spirit of Elijah Restored

Malachi 4:5-6 prophesies that the Spirit of Elijah will return before the great day of the Lord.

This spirit represents bold confrontation, prophetic clarity, and covenant restoration.

In the end-time Church, Elijah's spirit will operate through intercession, holiness, and fearless proclamation.

> "End-time believers will carry prophetic fire, not religious form."

5. The Apostolic and Prophetic Restoration

Ephesians 2:20 says the Church is "built on the foundation of apostles and prophets."

In the last days, these foundational ministries will be restored to bring structure, revelation, and order.

Apostolic authority governs expansion; prophetic authority governs direction.

> "When apostles and prophets walk in unity, the Church walks in authority."

6. Global Outpouring of the Spirit

Joel 2:28 *"I will pour out My Spirit on all flesh."*

This end-time outpouring is not limited by geography, denomination, or age.

Children, youth, and elders alike will operate in supernatural gifts.

Signs, wonders, and miracles will confirm the Gospel to every tribe and tongue.

> "The final revival will be the flood of God's glory covering the earth."

7. Authority Over Deception

Matthew 24:24 warns that false prophets and false christs will arise. Discernment will be essential.

True authority will always align with Scripture, exalt Jesus, and produce righteousness.

The Word will become the believer's compass; the Spirit, his interpreter.

> "Revelation without discernment leads to deception."

8. The Church as Heaven's Embassy

2 Corinthians 5:20 *"We are ambassadors for Christ."*

The Church is Heaven's embassy on earth, representing divine law amid earthly chaos.

Through intercession and decree, believers legislate Heaven's will over nations.

9. End-Time Warfare and the Overcoming Church

Revelation 12:11 *"They overcame him by the blood of the Lamb and by the word of their testimony."*

Victory in the last days will be secured not by fear or flight, but by faith and fortitude.

The Church will operate as an overcoming army - worshiping, warring, and witnessing in power.

> *"The end-time battle is not for survival but for supremacy."*

10. Authority in the Marketplace

End-time authority will extend beyond pulpits into **business, media, education, and government.**

Joseph, Daniel, and Esther are prototypes - believers placed in influence to govern with integrity.

Kingdom authority in these arenas will bring transformation and justice.

> *"The next revival will not stay in church buildings; it will invade nations and boardrooms."*

11. The Fearless Generation

Acts 4:13 describes the early apostles as bold, though "unlearned and ignorant men."

The end-time Church will carry that same fearlessness - a generation that knows its identity, walks in purity, and will not bow to culture or compromise.

12. Authority and the Glory Realm

Habakkuk 2:14 *"The earth will be filled with the knowledge of the glory of the Lord."*

Glory is the atmosphere of divine authority.

As believers walk in intimacy and obedience, the tangible presence of God will manifest — healing, delivering, and transforming.

> "The glory of God is the final frontier of authority."

13. The Marriage of the Lamb — Completion of Authority

Revelation 19:7–8 shows the Bride made ready - clothed in righteousness and glory.

When the Bride is mature, the Bridegroom will return.

The restoration of full authority in the Church precedes the return of Christ.

14. Reflection and Discussion

1. What distinguishes the end-time Church from the early Church?
2. How will apostolic and prophetic restoration prepare the Bride for Christ?
3. In what ways can believers exercise authority within society?
4. Why is discernment essential in this final age?
5. How can the Church remain fearless yet humble in rising darkness?

15. Practical Ministry Exercise
Prophetic Decree Session:

Students gather in prayer groups to intercede for nations, cities, and regions.

THE AUTHORITY OF THE BELIEVER

They will identify one area of cultural darkness (media, government, education, etc.) and release decrees of light and authority using Scripture.

Prayer Declaration:

"Father, we declare that the earth is Yours and the fullness thereof.

We take our place as Your Church; bold, pure, and full of power.

Let Your Kingdom come, Your will be done, and Your glory cover the nations.

Raise up a fearless Church that governs with love and truth.

We decree: Jesus Christ is Lord over the earth — now and forever. Amen."

Chapter Summary

- The end-time Church will operate in unprecedented power and purity.
- Apostolic and prophetic restoration will bring divine order and maturity.
- Global outpouring of the Spirit will manifest Kingdom authority worldwide.
- The Church will influence every sphere of society with light and truth.
- Christ will return for a victorious, radiant, and authoritative Bride.

Key Verse for Memorization

"The kingdoms of this world have become the kingdoms of our Lord and of His Christ, and He shall reign forever and ever."
Revelation 11:15

www.ingramcontent.com/pod-product-compliance
Lightning Source LLC
Chambersburg PA
CBHW032051150426
43194CB00006B/498